THE
CONSERVATORY
PLANNING·PLANTING
FURNISHING

Alan Toogood

WARD LOCK LIMITED · LONDON

Acknowledgements

The author and the publishers are most grateful to all those private conservatory owners who allowed us to photograph their conservatories and who also very kindly supplied us with information on how they use their conservatories. We are also grateful to the Royal Horticultural Society for allowing us to photograph a selection of plants at their Wisley Garden, and our thanks are due for the help and advice of those conservatory and greenhouse manufacturers whose products are featured in this book.

The publishers gratefully acknowledge the following for granting permission to reproduce colour photographs: Anthony Huxley (p.61); Syndication International Ltd (p.59); Amdega Ltd (p.109); Alexander Bartholomew Ltd (p.115); Room Outside Ltd (p.121 (lower)); and Machin Designs Ltd (p.121 (upper)). All the remainder of the photographs were taken by Bob Challinor and are copyright of Ward Lock Ltd.

All the line drawings are by Nils Solberg, except Fig. 7 which is by Ron Hayward.

© Ward Lock Limited 1985

First published in paperback in Great Britain in 1989.

Ward Lock Limited, 8 Clifford Street, London W1X 1RB, an Egmont Company.

House editor Denis Ingram
Layout by Melissa Orrom

Text filmset in Baskerville by Paul Hicks Limited and
Jamesway Graphics, Manchester

Printed and bound in Italy by
G. Canale and Co SpA

British Library Cataloguing in Publication Data

Toogood, Alan R. *1941–*
    The conservatory.– 2nd ed.
    1. Residences. Garden rooms.
    I. Title
    643'.55

ISBN 0-7063-6750-2

CONTENTS

PREFACE

In recent years there has been a revival of interest in conservatories, and indeed many new conservatory companies have become established, and are able to supply a wide choice of designs, from period to modern.

Conservatories enjoyed their greatest popularity in the Victorian era, but the idea pre-dates this by several centuries. Many of the Victorian conservatories were elaborate, both in design and in the layout of the interior. There was a swing away from the highly ornate at the start of this century to more simple designs.

But as far as conservatories today are concerned, people are becoming more adventurous again and one can see examples of quite elaborate conservatories in many private gardens. Today conservatories are often used as an extension of the living area: modern designs are comfortable, safe and within the pocket of many people. Putting up a conservatory can certainly be cheaper than moving house to gain more space and, what is more, provides an ideal environment for plants, these being much easier to grow under glass than in the rooms of the dwelling house, so long as suitable temperatures are provided.

I have planned this as an ideas book, rather than treating the subject on a 'how-to-do-it' basis. However, there are not only my own ideas in the book, but other peoples' also. I have visited privately owned conservatories and talked to the owners, to show you how conservatories can be used, both for living in and for growing plants.

The book is illustrated with many illustrations of the conservatories available today, to help you choose one that suits the style of your house and your needs. I have also included information on the materials used in construction – you may prefer a timber conservatory or one with an aluminium framework. Useful and essential equipment is also discussed.

You will find advice on siting a conservatory, planning permission, and erecting the structure. I have also put forward my ideas for laying it out internally, and how to landscape the outside.

Conservatory plants of all kinds for all-year round interest from flowers and foliage are described and illustrated, with hints on their cultivation. The difficult subject of matching plants' requirements with those of people has been covered, to enable you to choose suitable plants for living areas. It is of course desirable to display plants attractively and I hope that some of my ideas here will prove useful.

Of course, plants need care and attention if they are to flourish, so I have completed my book with a practical chapter on caring for plants throughout the year; it is important to care for plants correctly.

I very much hope that I can persuade you to invest in a conservatory, for I can assure you it will provide rather different and very enjoyable living conditions

A.T.

I

HISTORY AND DEVELOPMENT

What is a conservatory?

The original meaning of conservatory is a structure in which tender plants are 'conserved' in cold weather. John Evelyn, who was a well-known and knowledgeable writer on horticultural topics, first used the word in 1664, but he also applied it to greenhouses.

But by the late 18th century the two words – conservatory and greenhouse – had distinct meanings. It was accepted that the green-house was for propagating and growing tender plants, while the conservatory was a structure in which to display them attractively and to enjoy them. Plants such as flowering pot plants were raised in greenhouses and taken into the conservatory when they were in flower. When they had finished flowering they were taken back into the greenhouses.

Generally, conservatories have always been an integral part of the dwelling house, with access from a room, such as the drawing room or dining room. In the past they were often built with the house, not, as is often the case these days, added on as an afterthought.

A true conservatory is a glass structure with a glass roof, to allow maximum light transmission for the well-being of the plants. The framework is generally timber or aluminium alloy, but in the past was often cast iron or steel. The framework is built on a solid base, which may be brick or timber, to a height of about 1 m (3 ft).

The term 'lean-to greenhouse' also has to be considered in conjunc-tion with conservatories. But what is the difference between the two? This is very difficult to decide. A lean-to greenhouse, which is again built against the wall of the dwelling house, is like half of a free-standing greenhouse, with the roof sloping in one direction, the highest point being against a wall. Very often there is access from a room in the house to the lean-to. Generally, I think it is safe to say that a lean-to looks more like a conventional greenhouse whereas conservatories come in various styles, for example Victorian, Georgian or Gothic, and they vary enormously in shape: they may be in the shape of a septagon or octagon, for instance.

The lean-to greenhouse is generally 'hard up' against the house – in other words, it does not project a very great distance from the wall. Conservatories, on the other hand, often project far beyond the house: for example a conservatory could be a long structure at right-angles to the house wall.

Today the two terms – conservatory and lean-to greenhouse – very much overlap and there is no really clear definition. If you want to call your lean-to a conservatory, then by all means do so. There is nothing wrong in this, for a lean-to is used 'to conserve plants' in the same way as a more elaborate structure.

A brief history

Growing plants under cover goes back to Roman times. The Romans probably grew plants under thin sheets of mica and their structures were probably more like frames than greenhouses.

I will not dwell on the earliest forms of cultivation under cover but skip many centuries to the late 15th century as a starting point to the history of conservatories. Conservatories were undoubtedly a follow-on from orangeries, the earliest of which (about the late 15th century) were nothing more than heated 'sheds' for overwintering citrus fruits (mainly oranges), with no light in the winter for the plants. The plants were taken outside in the warmer weather.

The first use of glass in orangeries is recorded as early in the 17th century, in Heidelberg, Germany. Structures were gradually improved until by the late 17th century orangeries had larger windows but were still built with solid roofs.

Gradually people began to realise the importance of light for plants and glass was first used for roofs from the end of the 17th century. It was in that century also that gardeners started using the words greenhouses and conservatories for their 'plant houses'. Skipping a great deal of detail (so vast is the history of covered gardening that whole books have been written on the subject), suffice to say that structures were gradually improved, with the introduction of ventilation, for example. Experiments in design increased from the early 18th century, with increasing use of the lean-to structure against a wall.

Important plants grown under cover at about this time were citrus fruits, followed by pineapples, but by the early 19th century many ornamental tropical plants were being introduced to Britain and Europe by plant collectors. These were intrepid explorers, often risking their lives in steamy tropical jungles to bring back many of the plants that we are all so familiar with today. Much use was made of glass structures to grow these exotics.

Greenhouse structures were first used for 'entertainment' (or for living in as we say today) as early as the end of the 17th century. They were used in place of summer houses. It is recorded that in 1760 there was a privately owned glass structure (for citrus fruits) with access from the drawing room of the house.

The word conservatory (the modern meaning) was first recorded in a dictionary in 1782. There is another term, which is not often used today – the winter garden. This implied a really huge conservatory with access from the house, set out with large beds planted with trees, shrubs and other exotic plants, with paths between them to allow people to easily view the plants. The winter garden was virtually a 'covered garden', and very popular (with wealthy people) in the last century. Many of the grand houses of Europe had vast winter gardens, containing many of the new plants that were being brought back from the tropics.

This trend in the 19th century encouraged many other people to have conservatories, but on a more modest scale: the types that we are familiar with today, attached to the house and with access from a room. Again on a smaller scale many people had greenhouses for growing plants to 'furnish' their conservatories. Indeed, everyone who was anyone had a conservatory: it was considered an essential part of the social structure, and entertaining was the main role of this covered area, amid luxuriant plant growth.

Gardening writer Shirley Hibberd (1825–1890) wrote: 'A conservatory should be a garden under glass and a place for frequent resort and

Fig. 1. One of the outstanding conservatories of the 19th Century was Joseph Paxton's Great Conservatory at Chatsworth House. Unfortunately it had to be removed after the First World War.

7

agreeable assemblage at all seasons and especially at times of festivity'. From the 19th century all shapes of conservatory were built, such as dome-shaped, half-dome, curvilinear, hexagonal and octagonal. Often the interiors were laid out in the most elaborate manner, with pools, waterfalls, and so on, in typical Victorian extravaganza.

Glass making was also improved in the last century: glass was clearer allowing more light to enter the conservatory, and it was bedded in putty, perhaps with laps of lead or copper to exclude draughts and leaks.

As is well known, in the early part of the 20th century there was a swing away from the highly ornate and ostentatious Victorian garden to more simple natural gardening. Big estates disappeared and with them many of the grand Victorian conservatories. Many conservatories were pulled down simply because they proved too expensive to run and maintain. Also around this period it became clear that many plants would flourish in cooler conditions, and some even outdoors, so there was no need to provide steamy jungle conditions under glass.

Fig. 2. Mrs Beeton, in her *Dictionary of Everyday Gardening* (published in 1896), said the architectural style of a conservatory should be in harmony with that of the house. This pretty design for a ridge and furrow roof conservatory was, she suggested, suitable for a handsome villa residence.

As with so many good things in life, gardening under glass declined with the First World War. Interest recovered, though, between the wars, when small greenhouses became popular. The Second World War again put paid to ornamental gardening under glass and the emphasis was quite naturally on food production. Since the last war, mass-production techniques have allowed even more people to own greenhouses (including lean-to houses and conservatories), since they have brought down the prices to a realistic level. Indeed, in the last two decades the number of greenhouse owners has increased dramatically. From the late 1960s and early 1970s there has been renewed interest in conservatories for growing ornamental plants and for living in.

Today probably more people than ever before are buying conservatories and lean-to greenhouses to enlarge and improve their homes. I think this is partly due to the boom in house prices and the high cost of moving house. Instead of moving to larger houses, many people are spending money on improving and enlarging their present properties, and there are few better ways of doing this than investing in a conservatory. It seems to me the main use of a conservatory today is to provide living space, with the added bonus that it also ensures ideal conditions for plants.

The types and styles available today

Of course, various modern materials are used in present-day construction; for instance, aluminium and western red cedar have replaced cast-iron, steel and masonry. We have double glazing to conserve heat and excellent methods of glazing to ensure draught and leak-free structures.

We have a tremendous choice of structures, from the simple lean-to greenhouses to the most elaborate conservatories. We have lean-to versions of the traditional span-roof greenhouse, and a modern idea is the lean-to with curved eaves. There are lean-to versions of the mansard or curvilinear greenhouse with the roof panels set at various angles, which ensures extremely good light intensity.

We have a choice of lean-to greenhouses glazed virtually to the ground, or with solid sides to the height of benching or staging. Virtually any size required is available, with a choice of timber or aluminium alloy framework. Some aluminium models have an attractive white or bronze acrylic or anodized finish. In my opinion such lean-to structures look particularly good with modern houses.

The choice of conservatories today is enormous. There are very modern designs with large square or rectangular 'picture windows', an ideal choice for the modern house. If you have a period house there is an equally wide choice of styles: Victorian styles are proving very popular today and of course are ideal for Victorian houses and certain other period dwellings. There are Georgian styles available, and Gothic styles, the latter being particularly popular with city-house owners.

Although it is still possible – at a price – to have a conservatory designed from scratch and built on site, the more usual way today is to invest in a modular conservatory, but still designed for the customer's requirements. Manufacturers produce standardized units or modules to cut costs. These modules are fitted together in an infinite variety of designs. The customer gets the equivalent of a custom-built conservatory for about half the cost of a specially built model. That is why so many people these days can afford a large conservatory.

Generally they are built on a brick base or they may have a timber base. The specialist conservatory companies will advise on the style to suit your house – this is most important, for a Victorian-style conservatory is perhaps not the best choice for an ultra-modern house, nor a very modern-looking model for a period dwelling. Even the colour of the conservatory should be taken into account – perhaps a white conservatory would be a good choice for your house, or maybe natural cedarwood, to either blend or pleasantly contrast with the house.

2

CHOICE OF MATERIALS AND BUYING

Materials used in construction

The framework

We have a choice today of timber or aluminium alloy framework – that is, the glazing bars, etc, which hold the glass in place. Timber is the traditional material and there is no doubt that it blends in well with the surroundings and looks good with any style of dwelling house. Various kinds of timber are used by conservatory manufacturers, including western red cedar, which may be supplied with a cedarwood dressing to preserve it, but maintaining the natural colour; or primed ready for painting, white being the most popular colour for conservatories. The natural colour is 'warm' and looks particularly attractive with the older style of house.

European red pine is also used by some manufacturers and so, too, is mahogany, which is an expensive timber but has a long life.

Aluminium alloy has the advantage over timber in that it needs no preservation treatment. Many lean-to greenhouses these days are constructed of aluminium alloy, a material that blends particularly well with modern houses. One can opt for plain aluminium, or an acrylic, anodized or electrophoretic-paint finish, in bronze or white. Plain aluminium does look rather harsh and I much prefer a bronze or white finish.

The glass

Becoming more and more popular these days is double glazing for conservatories, which can give up to 50% reduction in energy loss and more effective temperature control, as well as muffling outside noise. Single glazing is still readily available, of course, and keeps down the cost of the conservatory.

Many conservatory manufacturers offer various sash designs in their modular conservatories, to match the architecture of the dwelling house. Generally toughened glass, 4 or 6 mm (0.16 or 0.24 in) thick, is used for glazing, and 7 mm (0.28 in) wire-reinforced safety glass is used by some manufacturers for the roof.

The walls

As I have already mentioned, the traditional conservatory is built on low walls, varying in height from 45 to 90 cm (18–36 in). Many conservatory manufacturers favour brick walls (or stone walls if it is felt these blend better with the house). However, one has the alternative choice of timber panelling for the walls. Many lean-to greenhouses have glass to ground level.

Doors and ventilators

Very popular are double doors, these being side hung in most conservatories, but in lean-to greenhouses or conservatories they may be sliding. In the more expensive conservatories brass door fittings are used.

Ventilation is provided by side sashes, top or side hung, and roof ventilators, which ideally should be operated by automatic ventilator openers.

Adding even more character

Manufacturers of the more expensive conservatories supply dentil mouldings, ridge cresting and finials in various period designs to match the style of the building. These may be timber, fibreglass or cast aluminium, and give the finishing touches to the building.

Buying a conservatory

Specialist manufacturers

As I have already indicated in my opening chapter, there is a number of specialist conservatory manufacturers who supply modular conservatories. These companies offer an excellent service and it is best to start off by requesting their brochures which give full specifications and show plenty of examples of their conservatories. Most of these companies advertise in the gardening press, and some of them exhibit at the Chelsea Flower Show and other large horticultural shows.

There are also company consultants available to give customers advice on the most suitable style for the house, and to assist with planning permission and building regulations.

Greenhouse and conservatory manufacturers

There are many more general greenhouse and conservatory manufacturers, who supply not only free-standing greenhouses, but lean-to types which are used as conservatories or garden rooms.

Most of them advertise in the gardening press and provide fully illustrated and very informative brochures. Again it is possible to obtain advice on suitability and styles of buildings and on planning permission.

It is possible to buy on a mail-order basis from many of these companies, and generally the conservatories are supplied in kit form for DIY assembly.

Display sites

Throughout the U.K. there are greenhouse display sites, often attached to garden centres, where one can see a wide range of conservatories from the general manufacturers. Not only can one compare the different makes, but also obtain advice from the site manager and his staff. Visits to your house can also generally be arranged. Manufacturers can indicate the nearest show site for their models. It does, of course, save on transport costs if you can buy from a local display site.

Additional equipment

There are a lot of accessories for conservatories, most of them optional extras. However, some are essential, such as shading blinds and staging, while others (e.g. fans and automatic ventilators) are not absolutely necessary but are well worth having.

Most conservatory and greenhouse manufacturers can supply these additional pieces of equipment, and there are also companies which specialize in various items, such as staging and conservatory blinds.

Staging

Staging is necessary for displaying pot plants and there is a very wide choice available, from the simple bench type to tiered staging on which you can build up impressive displays of plants. Staging is available in timber, such as western red cedar, or in aluminium, to match the framework of the conservatory.

There is a trend today towards 'flexible' staging that can be easily dismantled and re-arranged if you want to alter the layout of your conservatory. This type of staging is in aluminium, as timber staging does not readily lend itself to re-arrangement.

Much of this flexible staging consists of tubular aluminium framework fitted together with nylon joints. Shelving bars, often adjustable for various levels, hold plastic or aluminium capillary-watering trays and/or slatted timber or aluminium shelves. Often you can build up, out and along as required by adding more sections, as extension packs are available.

Automatic ventilator openers

There is no need to be on hand all day to open and close ventilators, for there is a wide range of automatic ventilator openers available, all very modestly priced. There are versions suitable for hinged ventilators and for louvre ventilators. It is virtually essential to have automatic openers in the roof as normally this is rather too high to reach easily.

Fans

Additional ventilation or air movement can be obtained by installing electric fans, either the circulating type, which keep the air moving, or extractor fans, which create a through-flow of cool air by pushing the warm air out of the conservatory. These are normally mounted in or near the roof.

There is also available a solar-powered extractor ventilator. It contains a solar photovoltaic cell which harnesses natural daylight to provide power for the electric motor which drives the fan.

The Eden Continental
conservatory, size 3.8 ×
2.2 m (12½ × 7½ ft),
belonging to Mrs G. W.
Williams (p.42). Note that
the structure is completely
glazed and does not take
light from the kitchen or
lounge.

The Banbury Classic
conservatory, with its
bronze and white finish
and translucent fibreglass
safety roofing, blends
beautifully with many
styles of architecture. This
one is owned by Mr and
Mrs A. V. Herbert (p.44)
and its size is 4.8 × 3 m
(16 × 10 ft).

Shading blinds

It is essential to have some form of shading to protect plants and people from strong sunshine. Roller blinds constitute the most suitable system for conservatories. There are many manually operated blinds available and you will find most greenhouse manufacturers supply them.

Blinds are available in various materials, such as wooden laths, plastic reeds, shading netting, woven polyethylene, white polythene sheeting, polypropylene netting and polyester material. However, there is no need to be on hand all day to raise and lower blinds as there are automatic systems available, and I would strongly recommend one of these as shade is provided only when it is needed.

There is a company in the U.K. who supply automatic, external, cedar-lath blinds. The laths are 2.5 cm (1 in) wide and 6 mm (¼ in) thick. The length and breadth of the roller blinds are made to suit individual conservatories and they can go down to ground level if required. The blinds are mounted on raised runners so that they do not interfere with ventilators.

The winding system is an electric motor controlled by adjustable electronic thermostat and light sensors. Shade is provided only when the light intensity and the temperature in the conservatory have reached their respective selected levels. Should either one of these controlling elements decrease below the critical level the blinds will be raised.

Another U.K. company supplies non-retractable aluminium louvre blinds for internal or external use. The white, perforated louvres can be tilted to any angle to exclude direct sunlight. Even when the blinds are fully closed the perforations allow a certain amount of filtered light to enter the conservatory. Fitted internally in a warm or tropical conservatory, the blinds will control light only, but fitted on the outside of a cool conservatory they will help to control light and heat.

Automatic watering

If you are away for quite a lot of the time you may find an automatic watering system useful. There are several systems available which run from the mains water supply via a header tank fitted with a ballcock valve. For large pots and containers there are various trickle and drip systems available, the water being applied *via* a system of spaghetti-like tubes from a main supply pipe.

For smaller pots on staging I like the capillary system of watering. Pot plants are placed on capillary matting which is kept moist. The water enters the pots via the drainage holes and rises up through the compost by capillary action. The plants take only the amount of water they require and therefore do not become too wet. In most capillary systems a constant-level water tray, fitted with a valve, is attached to the side of the staging to ensure the correct level of water is maintained.

Propagation facilities

As mentioned earlier, the ideal system is to raise plants in a separate greenhouse and to take them into the conservatory when they are

This superb timber-framed conservatory by Alexander Bartholomew Conservatories
Ltd. integrates well with the owners' Japanese rooftop garden, which commands a
panoramic view of the river Thames. The conservatory belongs to Dick and Tricia Power
(p.46) and is 4.8 × 3 m (16 × 10 ft) in size.

coming into flower. However, not everybody has a greenhouse and many people will be raising plants in their conservatory. In any event, wherever you propagate plants, a heated propagating case is strongly recommended for the successful raising of seeds and rooting of cuttings.

There are many to choose from, but for the conservatory I would suggest a propagator that looks attractive, rather than one that is purely utilitarian. Some of the larger, electrically heated propagating cases look like mini-greenhouses, having a glass or plastic top with sliding panels for access. These larger propagators can indeed be used as mini-greenhouses, for growing small plants which like very high temperatures and humidity – a form of Wardian case, in fact, which were popular in the Victorian period.

Heating is generally by means of an electrically heated base, the heating elements being sealed in and controlled by a thermostat.

If you intend doing a lot of propagation from cuttings then a mist-propagation unit is well worth considering, for with this even plants which are difficult to raise from cuttings can often be rooted. Basically, a mist unit provides bottom heat and keeps the leaves of the cuttings moist by intermittently misting them over with water.

However, the normal system of mist propagation, which is installed on an open bench, is not suitable for the conservatory, only for greenhouses which are used for propagation and growing.

There is available in the u.k., however, an enclosed mist propagation unit. It is an attractive circular propagator with misting facility and is electrically heated It is covered with a clear dome which has excellent ventilation facilities. Misting works at the press of a button, or it can be fully automated with an electronic controller kit which regulates misting frequencies according to light conditions. The higher the light intensity the more frequent the misting, for in these conditions the leaves of the cuttings dry off more quickly.

Ideally all propagation and plant raising should be confined to one part of the conservatory, perhaps providing a bench or staging specially for this, rather than scattering trays of seedlings and cuttings all over the place. After all, young plants are not particularly attractive and could detract from the displays of fully grown plants. Besides, young plants generally need more shade than larger specimens and this is more easily provided if they are all grouped together on the one bench. If you do not wish to shade the entire conservatory you can at least shade the plants growing on with, say, a piece of shading netting or muslin.

Control panels

To simplify electrical installations in a conservatory there are control panels available, from which you can run, say, lighting, a propagator and an electric heater. These fused control panels are connected to the mains electricity supply. Bear in mind that all electrical installations should be installed by a qualified electrician, and of course all electrical equipment must be of the type specially designed for conservatories and greenhouses – it will be waterproof and therefore completely safe.

3
PLANNING AND BUILDING

Having decided on the make, style and size of conservatory the next stage is to make sure you have a suitable site for it, to obtain all the necessary planning permission from your local authority and to decide on whether you want to erect it or employ the services of a specialist.

Choosing a site

Most people will want to build the conservatory against a wall of the house, ideally with access into the house, but one should try to avoid hiding an existing feature.

Do not think that a conservatory can be built only at ground level; some people, who live in town houses, have had elevated conservatories built on first-floor level. They are supported on 'stilts' or pillars. There are one or two conservatory companies who can design an elevated conservatory for you.

A conservatory need not be a single-storey structure, either. There are one or two instances of two-storey conservatories, with a staircase joining the upper and lower levels.

There are, of course, no hard and fast rules for siting a conservatory and indeed it does not have to be built on the wall of a dwelling house. There are many instances where people have built conservatories against free-standing garden walls, and very good they look, too, very much enhancing the garden.

Aspect

If possible, though, try to site a conservatory where it receives as much sun as possible. A south-facing wall is best in this respect, or failing that a west-facing wall would be almost as good. If you have no choice but to site the conservatory on a shady wall, such as one facing north or east, then do not despair, for there is a good range of plants that will survive in shady conditions. It will probably be more expensive to heat, though, for you will not be able to rely on the natural warmth of the sun.

Wherever possible try to make sure the site for a conservatory is sheltered from the wind, for cold winds can result in rapid heat loss and this means higher heating bills. If necessary ensure wind protection by planting a windbreak of, say, conifers, on the windward side, but well away from the conservatory to avoid shade. For instance, one may be able to plant a belt of fast-growing Leyland cypress, × *Cupressocyparis leylandii*. Strong-growing varieties of the Lawson cypress, *Chamaecyparis lawsoniana*, would also make a good windbreak, as would *Thuja plicata*. All of these conifers will form an effective windbreak within a few years.

Try to avoid siting the conservatory where it will be subjected to wind funnelling. This often occurs in the space between two houses, particularly if they are fairly close together.

You should also try to avoid erecting a conservatory where it will be overshadowed by large trees, for not only will these cast a great amount of shade, but leaves will collect on the roof and in the gutters, and dust and dirt will be washed down from the leaves by rain, creating a lot of grime on the glass. There is also the risk, of course, of falling branches. It is also worth mentioning here that it is a wise precaution to have a wire guard fitted along the eaves of the house roof to prevent tiles or slates falling onto the conservatory roof.

Planning permission and building regulations

It is essential to liaise with the planning department of your local authority when you are intending to build a conservatory.

Generally planning permission is not needed for conservatories as they come under permitted development. Permitted development includes extensions of up to 70 cubic metres (2472 cu ft) that are not on any wall fronting onto the highway. Extensions to listed buildings need consent, though. You must check with your local planning department to find out the situation regarding planning permission.

All conservatories on a house need approval under the building regulations, for the base/foundations and the structure itself must meet with standard specifications.

When you have decided on the make and size of conservatory, and have placed an order, the company will supply a plan and full specifications of the building in order for you to obtain planning permission and approval under the building regulations. At this stage contact your planning department. Many companies supply standard drawings for the base or foundations required.

All of this information must be submitted to your planning department, together with a scale plan of the site (house and garden with the proposed conservatory indicated, too).

If the conservatory is to be built over drains, manhole covers, etc, seek advice from your local authority, for building over these must comply with building regulations. For instance, manhole and inspection covers may have to be raised and drains reinforced.

The main thing is not to be afraid of the subject of planning permission and building regulations. Most conservatory companies will provide all the advice and information you need to get started, and some can even see the whole procedure through for you. You will also find your local authority very helpful in this respect – after all, it is in their interest to get things right. So do not be afraid to have an initial chat with your planning department, explaining to them exactly what you intend building, and they will then explain to you what you have to do.

The Banbury California conservatory's elegant flowing lines and attractive antique bronze finish enable it to blend in with many styles of architecture. Due to its shallow roof pitch and low ridge height it is an ideal choice for bungalows, yet there is plenty of headroom. This one is owned by Tony and Sheila Rees (p.44) and is approximately 3.6 m (12 ft) long and 2.4 m (8 ft) wide.

It is not possible to cover here all the rules and regulations concerning erecting a conservatory, for they do differ slightly from one part of the country to another.

Site preparation

The conservatory must, of course, be built on an adequate base, complying with building regulations. As a general guide, many conservatories will need a 10 cm (4 in) thick overall concrete slab laid on at least 10 cm (4 in) of hardcore. The concrete is thickened at the edges to a depth of at least 30 cm (12 in).

Then a damp-proof membrane is laid over this followed by a 5 cm (2 in) deep cement and sand screed.

Some companies, especially those who supply lean-to greenhouses, provide a prefabricated base, which could simply be positioned on concrete footings of a suitable depth, again laid on hardcore. Once again, the conservatory companies will advice on a suitable base and your local authority will advise on building regulations.

One has the choice of building the base oneself, or employing a local builder. It is likely that the base, and maybe the completed structure, will be examined by your local building inspector.

Erecting the conservatory

Some conservatory companies undertake site erection and glazing, while others may recommend an erection service. A local builder should also be able to erect the conservatory for you, following the manufacturer's instructions.

However, you may prefer to build the conservatory yourself, thereby saving labour costs. Some are easier to assemble than others. For instance, the modular conservatories, which come in sections, are fairly straightforward to put up. More difficult and certainly time-consuming are the metal-framed conservatories and lean-to greenhouses. These are supplied in kit form and there are many parts to assemble. However, step-by-step instructions are supplied, and these should be followed to the letter. The different components, e.g. glazing bars, are supplied in separate bundles or packages. I find it a good idea to thoroughly study the erection instructions before making a start, ensuring that I thoroughly understand them. It is certainly advisable to read through the instructions several times before making a start.

Timber-framed lean-to greenhouses and conservatories are easy to erect as they are supplied in sections which are simply bolted together. Sometimes the sections are already glazed, but this depends on the manufacturer.

Putting up a conservatory is, of course, much easier if two people are involved, and indeed for larger structures I would say it is essential to have two pairs of hands.

As soon as the conservatory has been erected, do not delay on any timber preservation treatment or painting, as recommended by the manufacturer. If the conservatory is to be painted, it will be delivered with a coat of priming paint, but even so final painting should be completed without delay. Framework in natural western red cedar will have been treated by the manufacturer, but I still like to apply another coat after erection.

Landscaping the outside

I feel that one should endeavour to blend the conservatory into the garden rather than having a sharp transition between building and garden. This is only a personal view, of course, but nevertheless you might find the following ideas helpful.

Building a patio

To my mind the best way to link the conservatory with the rest of the garden is to build a patio around it. There is available today a wide range of pre-cast concrete paving slabs in all shapes, sizes and colours. Personally I would choose some fairly neutral colour, like natural stone, buff or grey, rather than, say, green or pink. You should try to ensure, though, that the paving harmonizes with the dwelling house and the conservatory.

To be honest, though, there is really nothing to compare with natural stone, such as York paving. I know this is more expensive than pre-cast concrete slabs but it has a subtle quality that blends with buildings old and new. Concrete paving slabs are more in keeping in a modern setting.

For an old or period property brick paving might be more appropriate and would certainly be a suitable choice for Victorian houses. The paving could perhaps be matched up with the house bricks.

There are special hard paving bricks available but do avoid soft bricks, for frost can quickly break them up when laid as a patio. Stock bricks are also used for paving.

Bricks can be laid in various patterns, such as herringbone, or staggered like the bricks in the house walls. Bricks are best loosely laid rather than cementing them down as then they are easily replaced if they become damaged. Lay them flat, rather than on edge, and leave 9 mm (0.35 in) joints which can be filled by brushing sand into them.

Gravel has always been a popular surfacing material, from small Victorian terrace houses to stately homes. It looks good whether associated with modern buildings or with period architecture. Gravel areas can also look good with artificial paving slabs to provide a variation in texture. Pea shingle is the type to use with modern houses, spread to no more than 2.5 cm (1 in) deep, for if it is any deeper it is difficult to walk on. Pea shingle, though, does not look right in association with a Victorian house, for it is graded, and the Victorians used ungraded gravel. However, you cannot buy ungraded gravel today, so it would be a case of mixing together various graded gravels to obtain that ungraded look.

Marble might be considered if the conservatory is in a courtyard, and it is a good choice for city gardens. It is very expensive, of course. Marble for paving should have a honed surface rather than polished, as the former is non-slip.

The patio can meet up with the lawn, ensuring both are on the same level to make for easy mowing of the grass. However, if you use gravel it would be a better idea to surround the patio with small curbing stones to prevent the gravel spreading onto the lawn.

Plants in containers

One can extend the atmosphere of a conservatory out on to the patio by growing suitable plants in tubs, urns and other garden containers. Again there is a wide choice of containers: for instance, concrete or plastic, better suited to a modern setting; imitation stone urns and vases; timber troughs and tubs which look particularly good in a country garden; and terra-cotta pots and containers of all kinds, which look good in a period or contemporary setting.

Permanent or temporary plants can be grown in containers. For instance, you may opt for brightly coloured summer-bedding plants like zonal pelargoniums, petunias, ivy-leaved pelargoniums, fuchsias, begonias (both fibrous and tuberous rooted), and French and African marigolds. These could be followed by spring bedding plants like polyanthus, forget-me-nots, double daisies and pansies, and bulbs such as tulips and hyacinths.

There are many permanent plants for patio containers, which extend the tropical or sub-tropical theme from the conservatory into the garden. You might like to try the cabbage palm or *Cordyline australis*. This is not a true palm, but it is palm like in appearance, with narrow lanceolate leaves, greyish green, at the top of the stems. There is a variety called 'Purpurea' with purplish leaves. This plant is best for mild areas.

The only palm which is hardy in the u.k. is *Trachycarpus fortunei*, the Chusan palm, with a fibrous-coated trunk and large leaves carried in a cluster at the top. In milder climates other palms could also be grown in containers.

Phormiums, or New Zealand flax, also add a tropical touch to a patio with their erect sword-like leaves in various colours. They are hardy in all but extremely cold areas. With a similar habit are the yuccas, which also make excellent tub plants. There are numerous species and also variegated varieties.

There are not many really large-leaved shrubs suitable for growing outdoors all the year round in the u.k., but *Fatsia japonica* is an exception. This has large hand-shaped leaves, deep green and glossy, giving a decidedly sub-tropical touch to the patio. It flowers in the autumn, producing trusses of cream blooms.

Of course, the patio can also be used for standing outside during the summer some of your conservatory plants, particularly camellias, *Nerium oleander* and citrus fruits. (See Chapter 6 for further examples.)

A superbly designed half-octagonal conservatory from Room Outside Ltd. The gently curved tops to the window frames echo those of the ground floor of the house, integrating the two together, and the spacious patio forms an excellent link between conservatory and garden. This conservatory belongs to Mr and Mrs A. Johnstone (p.48) and is approximately 4.8 × 4.5 m (16 × 15 ft) in size.

This large Victorian-style conservatory is owned by John and Jilly Matthews (p.52) and was built by the previous owners of the house, winning for them a Homemaker of the Year Competition. The conservatory is 5.1 m (17 ft) long and 2.7 m (9 ft) wide.

A warm border

Some people extend the lawn almost up to the conservatory and have a border between it and the building in which to grow colourful bedding plants and other low-growing subjects. This can be an attractive way of tying in the conservatory with the garden. If the conservatory is sited against a south-facing wall, this should be a very warm border, ideal for growing some of the more tender perennial plants and bulbs all the year round, provided the soil is very well drained. Here you might try bulbs like nerines and eucomis, and perennials such as *Zauschneria californica*, with trumpet-shaped scarlet flowers; and silver-leaved plants like *Anthemis cupaniana* and the dwarf artemisias.

Alpines for a cool atmosphere

If you have a cool or unheated conservatory it might not look quite right creating a tropical or sub-tropical atmosphere on the outside, so here I would suggest growing alpines in containers in the patio. They look particularly attractive in old stone sinks, but the problem here is sinks are difficult to obtain and when they are located they are very expensive. Many people use instead old glazed sinks covered with a mixture of cement, sand and peat, known as hypertufa – it resembles natural tufa rock. The sinks should be raised slightly on brick supports.

Alpines or rock plants could also be grown in gaps between paving stones, or you could remove a few stones to allow for planting. Here we should choose the low-growing, carpet or mat-forming alpines, like raoulias and thymes. The latter do not mind if they are trodden on occasionally, when they give off their delightful fragrance.

These, then, are a few ideas for landscaping the area immediately surrounding the conservatory. Plenty of thought should also go into laying out the interior and I have outlined my ideas on this in the next chapter.

4

LAYING OUT THE INTERIOR

There is a great deal of enjoyment to be derived from choosing a conservatory and seeing it erected, but the most exciting part of all is laying out the interior. Here I am touching on a very personal subject for you will no doubt have your own ideas for floor coverings, furnishings and so on. However, I can but put forward ideas, some of which you may like to consider.

Of course, the way in which a conservatory is laid out will depend very much on the way in which you intend using it. A conservatory to be used mainly as a living or working area could well be very different from one used primarily for growing and displaying plants. In the former instance the interior would probably resemble more the rooms in the house, but in the latter case the interior would need to be laid out in a more practical way, with a floor surface that could take water, and the emphasis being on staging and other aids for displaying plants rather than on furnishings.

The floor

This will almost certainly be the first consideration, the floor covering being determined on how you intend using the conservatory. The conservatory, as discussed in Chapter 3, will almost certainly be built on a substantial concrete base, finished off with a smooth cement and sand screed, so this gives an excellent base for ornamental floor coverings.

Floor coverings for living areas

I have often seen pre-cast concrete paving slabs used in conservatories and they can certainly be most attractive. Here the coloured slabs come into their own – they look far better in a conservatory than in the garden. You could perhaps use two different colours, creating a chequer-board effect: say grey and green, or grey and pink. These are best laid on mortar with 6 mm (¼ in) joints which can later be grouted, perhaps with coloured mortar if desired, making sure the grouting is slightly below the level of the slabs. I would suggest you try to obtain non-slip paving slabs: indeed some have a most attractive textured surface.

It is not always a good idea to use the smallest slabs, unless you have a very tiny conservatory. For most structures 60 cm (2 ft) square slabs give a more pleasing, less fussy effect.

Inside view of a spacious Edwardian conservatory, belonging to Denis and Audrey Hayes (p.56). The conservatory is 6 × 4.2 m (20 × 14 ft) in area and was built *c.* 1905. Note the long-lasting quarry tiles on the floor and the attractive stone-facing to the inside of the walls, which are 1 m (3 ft) in height. The rockery at the far end (left) incorporates a small pool.

Quarry tiles look good anywhere and can be used with virtually any style of building. They are often a pleasing heather colour and have a non-slip surface. They are laid in the same way as pre-cast concrete paving slabs but with smaller joints, which are again grouted.

Marble is a luxurious flooring for conservatories and helps to create a cool atmosphere. Also it is probably the most expensive material available for creating a conservatory floor. Square marble slabs, though, do indeed look most attractive, and of course you could use two colours if desired to give a chequer-board effect. Do not choose polished marble, though, for this is inclined to be rather slippery, especially when wet. Marble paving should have a honed surface, which is non-slip.

Mats can, of course, be placed on hard surfaces such as concrete paving slabs, quarry tiles and marble slabs – I particularly like rush mats which are available in various sizes and shapes. Mats can also be used on vinyl floor tiles, which are another suitable covering for conservatory floors. There is a wide choice of colours and designs and one can, if desired, lay an attractively patterned floor with these. They are extremely hard-wearing and are easily cleaned. Water will not harm them, either. Vinyl tiles are easily laid, using one of the special adhesives available.

As I mentioned above, I am very fond of rush matting in conservatories. This could be used to cover the entire floor, from wall to wall. It can, of course, be laid direct on the smooth cement screed, but first I would suggest treating this with a cement sealant to prevent a dusty surface. Suitable sealants are obtainable from DIY stores, builders' merchants, etc.

Try not to wet the matting, for I find that this results in unsightly marks. Rush matting gives a 'warmer' floor yet is very hardwearing. It is available in various colours, natural as well as shades of brown, etc.

You may prefer to have carpeting in your conservatory and here I would suggest cord carpeting as being the most suitable. It is rather hard on bare feet, but is extremely hardwearing. Again it can be laid on the sealed screed, but in this instance perhaps with a soft underlay. As with rush matting, try not to get this wet – treat it as you would your lounge carpet. As with other kinds of carpeting, there are many colours to choose from.

The floor in the plant conservatory

If the conservatory is to be used for growing plants rather than for living, then you probably need do nothing more than seal the cement screed to prevent a dusty surface. Then you can splash water around to your heart's content. However, if you still want a more attractive floor then lay pre-cast concrete slabs or quarry tiles.

In order to relieve a large expanse of concrete, you could create some gravel areas on which to stand plants, perhaps, or maybe under the staging. The gravel will help to provide a humid atmosphere if it is kept moist. The gravel could be contained by small concrete curbing stones, but make sure you leave some small gaps between some of them to allow any excess water to escape. You could use pea shingle for these areas, or one of the horticultural aggregates.

Beds for planting

If you have a reasonably large conservatory you might like to consider constructing soil beds in which to grow plants, an idea much favoured by the Victorians. There is no doubt that plants grow much better in beds than in pots, so much so that shrubs, climbers and other plants could quickly become too large. However, the way to overcome this problem is to choose plants of a suitable size for your conservatory. In my opinion plants look far more natural in soil beds than in pots.

Concerning the construction of soil beds, we have a slight problem if the conservatory is built on a concrete slab; the answer is to build raised beds, but this is no bad thing as they can look most attractive.

However, provision can be made at the outset for soil beds in the conservatory by simply leaving the appropriate areas unconcreted. Care must be taken, of course, to ensure that these areas do not encroach on the foundations. Where soil beds are constructed on existing garden soil, the initial preparation involves digging to two depths of the spade (double digging), breaking up the subsoil well to assist in drainage, and adding bulky organic matter to each trench, such as well-rotted farmyard manure or garden compost.

Beds can be any shape desired – maybe formal, such as square or rectangular, or informal, of irregular shape. They may be made around the edges of the conservatory or even in the centre if the building is sufficiently large, maybe with paths running through them. There are various materials you could use to construct paths – I like circular pieces of tree trunk, about 7.5 cm (3 in) thick, laid as stepping 'stones'. They are sunk into the soil so that their surfaces are level with the soil surface. Paths can also be made from a coarse grade of pulverized bark, from pea shingle or from one of the horticultural aggregates.

Raised beds are quite easily constructed and they can even be terraced, with several levels rather like wide steps. Building up can be accomplished with logs or natural stone, or indeed with any material that takes your fancy, such as bricks or ornamental walling blocks.

Do not build beds hard up against the structure, or you will have problems with dampness penetrating the timber. If a bed is to be built near a side of the conservatory it would be better to build a low brick wall at the back, with adequate space between it and the conservatory wall. If the conservatory is built on a low brick wall then you will not have this problem.

You will need a reasonable depth of soil in which to grow plants about 45 cm (18 in) will be sufficient. Build up the beds with good-quality topsoil, light to medium loam if possible.

If desired, a few well-shaped pieces of rock could be included in the bed, over which low-growing and trailing plants can scramble. The rocks should be partially sunk in the soil.

After planting, the surface of the bed could be mulched with a suitable material to give a pleasing finish. I rather like pulverized bark for mulching, a layer 5–7.5 cm (2–3 in) deep being sufficient. If you are growing cacti in the bed use a layer of coarse sand or gravel.

Staging for pot plants

As mentioned in Chapter 2, staging need not be a permanent fixture and if you buy the type that can be easily dismantled you can change the layout according to your requirements.

The tiered staging is, of course, designed for positioning against a wall, such as the back wall of the conservatory. Ordinary staging, the bench type, is generally best arranged around the sides of the conservatory, keeping the centre clear for furniture, etc. However, if the conservatory is sufficiently large you may wish to consider having some staging in the centre: perhaps two sets of tiered staging could be used here, placed back to back to give you almost a pyramid-shaped arrangement for displaying plants.

Do not forget that shelving is also available and can be useful for displaying pot plants, especially trailing kinds, on the back wall. There are also special fittings available for putting up shelving in the roof area, again a good way of displaying trailing plants, and also useful in a propagating area for trays of seedlings which need maximum light.

Constructing a pool

A pool can make a beautiful feature in a conservatory (see Chapter 6) and these days is very easy to construct, using one of the special pool liners, rather than the old-fashioned method of lining the excavation with concrete.

The pool can be any shape you desire: in a formal setting it is probably best to choose a regular shape such as square, rectangular or circular. However, in a more natural setting, say in a bed planted with shrubs and other tender plants, an informal shape would be a better choice, with gently curving edges.

The most natural-looking effect is achieved when the pool is sunk into the ground, with the water level at or just below ground level. But a raised pool can also be effective and is particularly suitable in a formal setting. It could be incorporated into the paved area. This is probably more easily constructed, too, for you will not have to excavate, but build it up with ornamental walling blocks or bricks. The advantage of a ground-level pool, though, is that you will be able to plant moisture-loving plants around the edge.

If waterlilies are to be grown in the pool, and you wish to introduce some fish, then it should be at least 45 cm (18 in) deep.

To construct a ground-level pool, first excavate a hole to the shape desired, with the sides sloping very slightly inwards. You may wish to grown marginal plants in shallow water around the edge of the pool, in

This lily pool and waterfall forms the centre piece of a magnificent 12 m (40 ft) square atrium (covered courtyard), belonging to Mr and Mrs J. van Zwanenberg (p.63). The pool contains blue tropical waterlilies and is surrounded by lush foliage plants like this variegated hibiscus, monstera and rubber plant.

The double pool in this luxurious conservatory belonging to David and Gill Cons (p.50) verges on the *trompe l'oeil*. It seems as though there is one pool extending from the inside to the outside; in fact there are two pools separated by the conservatory wall. Fish in both add to the enjoyment of this feature; the pool's edge is surrounded by lush ferns, begonias and peperomias.

which case while you are excavating you should form a 20 cm (8 in) wide ledge around the pool. Containers of marginal plants can then be placed on this. Most of them need only a few inches of water over their roots so take this into account when forming the shelf, allowing for the depth of containers.

A pool can be lined with butyl-rubber pool liner, which has a life of a great many years. Cheaper, and with a shorter life, are heavy-gauge plastic or PVC liners. Generally these need renewing after several years.

Liners can be bought in any size from aquatic specialists and mould to the shape of the excavation as water is added. When ordering a liner, state the size of your pool – the length, width and depth. Catalogues supplied by aquatic specialists tell you how to calculate the size of liner required.

Before introducing the liner, line the excavation with a layer of soft builders' sand to prevent stones or other debris from piercing the liner. Then the liner is laid over the excavation and water added. You will see that it gradually moulds to the shape you have created.

The edge of the liner should extend over the edges of the pool. Do not be tempted to cut it, but hide it with an edging of paving slabs, crazy paving, rocks or even soil.

Raised pools, built of walling blocks or bricks, can be lined in the same way, but do make sure that the inner surfaces are smooth – rough

Fig. 3. A raised pool is the easiest means of providing a water feature in a conservatory. If the conservatory is unheated then hardy aquatic plants should be chosen. However, if adequate warmth can be provided, many fascinating tender plants will thrive, including tropical waterlilies (nymphaea species), *Cyperus alternifolius*, the water hyacinth (*Eichhornia crassipes*), and the water lettuce (*Pistia stratiotes*).

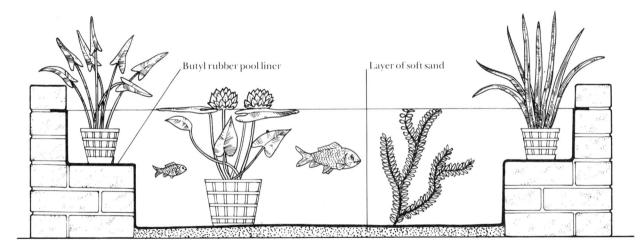

Butyl rubber pool liner   Layer of soft sand

mortar could pierce the liner. And place a layer of soft builders' sand in the bottom. The edges of the liner in this instance can be hidden by a final course of bricks, walling blocks or with coping stones.

There is yet another way of constructing a pool, and this is to use one of the pre-fabricated fibreglass or plastic pools, stocked by many garden centres. These pools are simply placed into a hole of suitable size and shape, making sure they are completely level, and packing the sides firmly with soil to prevent any movement. The edges of these pools are hidden as suggested for flexible liners. They work out more expensive than flexible liners and of course you have to choose one of the shapes that are available, which may not suit your requirements. However, they generally come with ready formed shelves for placement of marginal plants in containers.

If you want to be really ambitious you may like to construct a waterfall to run into the pool. Again there are ready-formed waterfall units available from garden centres, or you could use a strip of pool liner. The waterfall could start from a small pool in a rock garden alongside or at the back of the main pool. The water is circulated by means of a submersible electric pump, a wide range of these being supplied by water-gardening specialists, and by many garden centres. However, bear in mind that waterlilies do not like moving water, so would not really appreciate a waterfall. Fish, on the other hand, would delight in the well-oxygenated water.

This all sounds very ambitious – shades of the grand Victorian conservatories. Yet these days it is all very simple to create and indeed I know of several examples of waterfalls and pools in other people's conservatories. Water gardening is enjoying great popularity out of doors, so why not in the conservatory?

Supports for climbing plants

Many plants recommended in Chapter 6 require supports of some kind, for they are climbers. Some of the fruits, too, like grapes and peaches, need supporting.

Most plants can be trained to a system of horizontal wires, spaced from 20 to 30 cm (8 to 12 in) apart, on the back wall or even on the sides of the conservatory, and if necessary taken up into the roof area.

Use heavy-gauge galvanized or plastic-coated wire. There are all kinds of fittings available for wires. There are special plugs or fittings available from several companies for securing wires in metal-framed conservatories. For fixing them to timber framework there are metal eye hooks which are screwed into the woodwork. There are wall nails or 'vine eyes' for securing wires to the back wall. All of these ensure the wires are an inch or two from the wall, to allow for air circulation behind the plants. Plants are tied in with soft garden string or raffia.

Ornamental plants could also be trained to trellis work fixed to a wall. There is a wide range of trellis panels available in various shapes and sizes. You may opt for wooden trellis, or the more modern plastic-coated steel trellis. Suitable fittings or brackets are available to secure the panels an inch or two from the wall.

There are even small trellis panels available for plants growing in pots; and also for pot work, ordinary bamboo canes make good supports for small climbing plants.

Many plants, such as some of the philodendrons, can be grown up moss poles. These are ideal for those plants which produce aerial roots, for these grow into the moss and help to support the plant.

A moss pole can be used in a pot or in a soil bed and is very easily

Fig. 4. Moss poles are easily made at home as shown here, although proprietary versions are available. They make ideal supports for climbing plants which produce aerial roots from their stems, such as the philodendrons, and the Swiss Cheese plant or *Monstera deliciosa*. The roots will grow into the moss, which should be kept moist at all times.

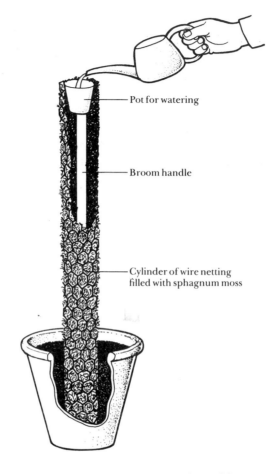

Pot for watering

Broom handle

Cylinder of wire netting filled with sphagnum moss

made. Use a broom handle of suitable length and insert this well into the soil. Place over this a cylinder of small-mesh wire netting, extending it below the soil surface. Then pack the cylinder with live sphagnum moss, which you should be able to obtain from a florist. A small pot can be inserted in the top of the wire cylinder and rested on the top of the broom handle. This provides an easy means of keeping the moss moist – simply pour water into the pot and it will trickle down through the moss. If you do not use this method, keep the moss moist by spraying it as necessary with a hand sprayer.

If you want to make a taller and thicker moss column, then use a wooden fencing post or tree stake. This would provide a more adequate support for larger plants.

A plant tree for epiphytes

In the lists in Chapter 6 you will see that some plants are epiphytic, especially many of the bromeliads. This means that in the wild they grow on trees (or occasionally on rocks). Many epiphytes will grow well

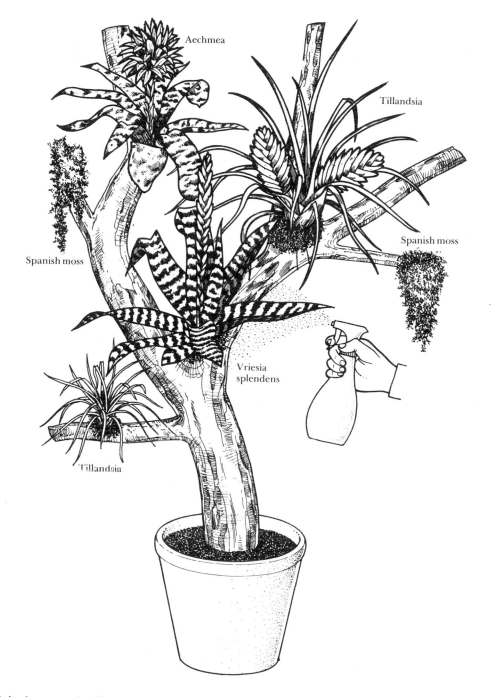

Fig. 5. Epiphytic or tree-dwelling plants are best grown and displayed on a plant tree. This can be made from a section of tree or from a suitably branched tree branch. The plant tree can be any size desired and can either be secured in a pot or in a soil bed. Here, bromeliads are being grown on a tree. Plants are watered by regularly spraying them and the tree with water.

enough in pots, but they look more natural if grown on a dead tree or a piece of branch. The air plants or atmospheric tillandsias will not grow in pots and have to be mounted on wood of some kind. The reason is that they produce few, if any, roots and if grown in pots of compost they are liable to rot off.

In any case, a tree bearing a collection of bromeliads and other epiphytic plants makes a stunning feature in the conservatory. The idea comes from the U.S.A where this method of growing is popular. It is gradually catching on in other countries as people come to realize how attractive a plant tree can be. Some garden centres are now displaying plants in this way and examples can also be seen in botanic gardens.

The tree can, of course, be any height required, from perhaps 1 m (3 ft) to almost the height of the conservatory roof. The tree should be dead but perfectly sound – in other words, not starting to rot. I use the term tree, but generally one would use a tree branch, ideally one that is well-branched. But where does one obtain a tree branch? On no account chop one off a tree in the countryside. You may be permitted to take a fallen tree branch but you must seek permission first. Or there may be some tree pruning or felling going on in your locality – perhaps in a park or neighbour's garden. Ask if you can have a branch.

The tree should be inserted firmly in a soil bed, reasonably deeply, ramming the soil all round it. The part of the tree below soil level should be treated with **horticultural** timber preservative. If you do not have a soil bed, use a pot of suitable size. The tree is positioned in the centre and the pot filled with mortar. Do not use soil or the tree will not be sufficiently firm.

There are various ways of securing plants to a tree. You could fix small specimens to separate pieces of bark before setting them on the tree, as this will allow you to move them around if desired. Larger, heavier plants, however, are best fixed directly on the tree. Maybe you can wedge them in the crotches of branches, or make small planting pockets with pieces of bark or cork bark nailed to the tree. These can be filled with suitable compost.

If plants are supplied in pots, remove them and tease away some of the compost before securing them to the tree. Surround the roots with sphagnum moss to hold the compost in place. It is far better to use live sphagnum moss rather than dead, as the former is green.

On no account place compost or moss around the roots of the air plants or atmospheric tillandsias, (if indeed they have any roots) or the plants will rot.

The plants can be secured to the tree or to pieces of bark with thin nylon string or with copper wire or plastic-coated wire. Do not tie them on too tightly, though, or the tying material may cut into the plants. Such tying materials can also be used to hold in sphagnum moss around the roots.

The plants are watered by spraying the entire tree with water. I think you will find that epiphytic plants grow much better on a tree and they are certainly easier to maintain.

An inside view of this delightful timber-framed, half-octagonal ended conservatory supplied by Alexander Bartholomew Conservatories Ltd. for Chris Albert (p.46). The conservatory is used both for relaxing in and, as it adjoins the kitchen, for taking meals in. Note what an excellent choice cane furniture is for a conservatory as it blends so well with the plants.

Hanging containers

A good way of displaying trailing or pendulous plants is in hanging containers, perhaps fixed in the roof of the conservatory. However, there are available all kinds of ornamental brackets which can be used to support hanging containers on the walls. I particularly like black wrought-iron brackets for this purpose.

There are several kinds of hanging container, the best-known being hanging baskets. There are two kinds of basket, the traditional galvanized-wire type (or plastic-coated in more modern versions) and the moulded plastic type. Often the latter have a built-in drip tray. Wire baskets are lined with sphagnum moss before planting. I would suggest that the moulded plastic baskets are more suitable for the 'lived-in' conservatory as there is no risk of drips when watering.

There are other kinds of hanging container including pots, in terra-cotta, ceramic or plastic.

Pots of trailing plants can also be displayed on wall trellis. There are available special brackets which support pot holders and these are designed for the modern plastic-coated steel trellis. Not enough use is made of walls for displaying pot plants – the idea is more popular in the U.S.A. – yet it can be most effective.

Heating the conservatory

Temperatures will be discussed in Chapter 7 so here I will consider the various methods of heating a conservatory. Wherever possible I would suggest running the domestic heating system into the conservatory as this would surely provide the most economical means of heating. However, this would not be suitable for a conservatory devoted only to plants, where there may be a lot of moisture.

If it is not possible to run in a domestic system then an independent heating system will have to be considered. One has a choice of gas or electric heaters, paraffin heaters or a boiler system with hot-water pipes. There are many companies who supply heaters specially designed for greenhouses and conservatories. I would emphasise it is best to use a heater designed for horticultural use, especially if there is a lot of moisture in the conservatory.

Electric heaters

Electricity is an excellent choice for it is clean, efficient, reliable, automatic and generally convenient. Electricity gives off dry heat so a dry atmosphere will be created.

However, it is a very expensive fuel, as we all know, but heaters have thermostatic control for economical running. Remember you should employ a qualified electrician to install the electricity supply.

There are various kinds of electric greenhouse heater, including fan heaters. The consist of a small portable cabinet with a fan and heating element, and warm air is blown out. They have the advantage of keeping the air moving. Do not allow a fan heater to blow directly onto plants.

Tubular heaters consist of hollow tubes, inside of which are heating elements. They are generally installed in banks along the sides of the conservatory. I consider they are very neat and compact.

Convection heaters are basically cabinets with heating elements inside to warm the air. As the warm air rises out of the top of the cabinet, so cool air is drawn in at the bottom. Like fan heaters, the convection type keeps the air moving. Convection heaters are particularly recommended for large conservatories.

Gas heaters

Gas heaters are very popular for heating conservatories and green-houses. If you have a supply of natural gas, then buy a natural-gas type of heater. This would be cheaper to run than bottled gas. A gas heater is basically a warm-air cabinet and is thermostatically controlled. Gas gives off carbon-dioxide, which is beneficial to plants, and also gives off water vapour which will prevent the atmosphere from becoming too dry. You will need to employ a professional gas engineer to install the gas supply and connect up the heater.

Heaters which run off bottled gas are similar but they are portable. Again one has thermostatic control. They run off propane or butane gas and need the minimum of attention and maintenance. You will find that buying large gas cylinders rather than small ones is more economical.

Paraffin heaters

I am not altogether convinced that paraffin heaters are the best means of heating a conservatory, although they are certainly more efficient than they used to be. Most are really only adequate for keeping a conservatory frost free, not for maintaining high temperatures, and therefore are perhaps better suited to normal greenhouses, where they are widely used.

Thermostatic control is available on some models. There are two basic types: the blue-flame heater, with less risk of fumes being produced, and the yellow-flame heater, which is almost as good as the former. Advantages are that paraffin heaters are comparatively cheap to buy and run, are portable, and give off carbon-dioxide, which is appreciated by plants.

There are several disadvantages, though: they need frequent atten-tion; a lot of water vapour is produced, resulting in condensation; some ventilation must be given at all times; and they can give off harmful fumes (harmful to plants) if not regularly cleaned.

Some models can be fitted with pipes or ducts to distribute the heat more efficiently. Always use high-grade paraffin and avoid placing the heater in a draught.

Boiler systems

A boiler and hot-water pipes is, of course, an old-fashioned method of heating, but modern systems are very efficient and need minimum attention. Such a system is ideal for a large conservatory and where high temperatures are required. The boiler, which must be under cover outside the conservatory, can be fired by solid fuel, oil or mains gas. Solid fuel is recommended if you want to maintain high temperatures with realistic running costs. You have automation, of course, if you opt for oil or gas. Minimum attention is needed, however, even with solid fuel. Hot-water pipes, which run around the walls, give out dry heat.

There are one or two disadvantages: a boiler system does not respond very quickly to temperature changes, it is rather bulky, and there will be daily stoking and ash clearing if solid fuel is used. The suppliers will advise on size of boiler and necessary pipe length for your conservatory, according to the temperature you wish to maintain.

Size of heater required

The heat output must be sufficient to maintain the temperature you require in your size of conservatory. You will find that most heater manufacturers/suppliers will advise on this, if you state the size of your conservatory and the temperature range you wish to maintain. Generally, a heater should have a slightly higher output than needed, to be sure that it can cope in periods of really severe weather.

Lighting

Obviously some form of lighting will be needed and can be provided by means of fluorescent tubes fitted in the roof area.

There are also various kinds of decorative lighting available these days, designed for use in conservatories. For instance, one can illuminate an ornamental plant display at night. Spot lights can be used, perhaps to highlight plants which have especially attractive leaves, or which have a spectacular flower display.

You must make sure that lighting systems are specially designed for conservatory use, and have them installed by a qualified electrician.

Furniture

Here again, as with floor coverings, I am coming onto a very personal subject, for what appeals to one person may certainly not appeal to another. However, I think it is safe to say that ordinary sitting-room/lounge furniture is not generally used in a conservatory. There is available from garden centres, large stores, etc, a very wide range of furniture which is more appropriate for use in a conservatory.

Tables and chairs can be obtained in cast aluminium, intricately patterned, resembling the cast-iron furniture of times past. Usually they are painted white. Or you may prefer timber tables and chairs; again the kinds designed for garden use look very good in a conservatory. They may be made from cedarwood, or various tropical woods.

I am particularly fond of cane furniture and one can obtain tables and chairs in this. To me it seems a natural choice for the conservatory, perhaps because it is a natural material and associates well with plants.

There is also a very wide choice of tubular aluminium furniture and this looks particularly attractive in a modern setting. Sometimes it is plastic-coated.

If you want a bit more comfort when relaxing I would suggest the upholstered garden/conservatory chairs. Often these come in brightly patterned materials, but it is possible to obtain more subtle colours. Generally this type of chair folds up for easy storage.

I would therefore suggest you have a good look around garden centres and department stores before making a choice, for there is such a wide range of suitable furniture available today.

Decorating the back wall

I think it is often a good idea to paint the back wall of the conservatory a light colour to help reflect light, especially if it is brickwork. If it is rendered then the normal practice anyway is to paint the entire house walls.

If the house walls are already painted, you will probably want to use the same colour inside the conservatory. If not, then I would suggest you use white or cream, whichever matches up best with the framework of the conservatory. Use a good-quality masonry paint: the modern ones which contain fine sand are very long lasting and some of them give a textured finish.

Statuary

You either like statuary or hate it. If it is very good quality I like it in a garden, and especially in a conservatory, to create a focal point. There is something rather charming about a white figure surrounded by or peering through lush foliage. I am not saying one should overdo it, but one or two choice pieces can create a great deal of atmosphere. If I could afford it I would choose an antique garden statue, perhaps in marble, or bronze, but do not dismiss modern statuary, perhaps in reconstituted stone. Some pieces are extremely well produced. In a very modern setting there would no doubt be a place for a piece of abstract sculpture.

The Chelsea Flower Show in London is one place to see high-quality garden statuary, where some of the leading sculptors exhibit.

5

OTHER PEOPLE'S CONSERVATORIES

All private conservatory owners have their own ideas for laying out, using conservatories and for displaying their plants.

The publishers and I have been very fortunate in being allowed to visit some of these private conservatories, so that I am able to describe and illustrate other people's ideas. Here you will find a diversity of sizes from a modest 2.4 × 2.4 m (8 × 8 ft) to a Roman-style atrium (in effect a covered courtyard) 12 × 12 m (40 x 40 ft) in area. The various photographs illustrate how conservatories can be used, both for living in and for growing plants. Also, hidden away in these private domains is a wealth of interesting plants.

Standard designs

ROBERT AND BARBARA OSBORN
of Horley, Surrey

Robert and Barbara Osborn invested in a 2.4 by 2.4 m (8 by 8 ft) Florada conservatory to provide extra space. It is an attractive conservatory in aluminium with a bronze finish and curved eaves. Pleasant evenings are spent here, and meals enjoyed, and Robert also uses it as a study.

Heating in the winter is by means of a portable Calor-gas heater.

Robert and Barbara particularly like foliage plants and have a tall Swiss cheese plant and a weeping fig, as well as smaller plants like chlorophytums or spider plants. Barbara is also interested in cacti and intends to invest in some reasonably large specimens which will, of course, flourish in this cool conservatory.

MRS G. W. WILLIAMS
of Merrow, near Guildford, Surrey

Mrs Williams says her Eden Continental, 3.8 by 2.2 m (12½ by 7½ ft) conservatory is the best investment she has ever made and gives her a great deal of enjoyment.

The aluminium framework is completely glazed and does not take light from the kitchen or lounge.

Mrs Williams' conservatory is very much a living area, well-furnished with a relaxator chair, tables, chairs and bookcase. Most meals are taken there and it is even used for sleeping visitors. Plants also share the

One could not have chosen a better conservatory for this style of house for the bronze finish blends beautifully with the architecture. The conservatory is a Florada one, owned by Robert and Barbara Osborn, who use it both as a study and as a place to relax in. Here Barbara enjoys the afternoon sunshine on the patio with her daughter, Eleanor. Size of conservatory: 2.4 × 2.4 m (8 × 8 ft).

Mrs G. W. Williams is very pleased with her Eden Continental conservatory – being fully glazed it does not take light from the adjoining rooms, and provides an ideal environment for relaxing in and for growing favourite plants.

conservatory with Mrs Williams, including rubber plants, dracaenas, pelargoniums and other house plants. Mrs Williams says it brings back memories of the tropics – the West Indies – where she and her husband used to live.

TONY AND SHEILA REES
of Witley, Godalming, Surrey

With two teenage children – Rebecca and Jonathan – Tony and Sheila Rees were thinking of moving as they needed more space. However, they found this rather expensive and so decided to create more space by investing in a Banbury California conservatory, which is about 3.6 m (12 ft) long and about 2.4 m (8 ft) wide. This aluminium conservatory has attractive curved eaves and the framework a pleasing bronze finish.

The conservatory fits neatly into an L-shape formed by the house and access is from the kitchen. The conservatory is kept just frost free in the winter with the aid of an electric fan heater. Anglepoise lights enable use to be made of it at night.

The conservatory is used as a living area and most meals are taken there during the summer. The conservatory is used for plants mainly during the winter, many being grown in pots and tubs and kept outside during the summer.

Plants include fuchsias (including a fine standard fuchsia), 1.2 m (4 ft) high orange trees, and a Passion flower. Stephanotis is also grown, and there is a fine white summer-flowering jasmine growing up one wall. A bougainvillea will be added soon for its brightly coloured bracts.

Hanging baskets provide colour in the summer and are planted with thunbergia, ivy-leaf pelargoniums and trailing fuchsias.

MR AND MRS A. V. HERBERT
of Lightwater, near Bagshot, Surrey

Mr and Mrs Herbert invested in the smart bronze and white finished aluminium Banbury Classic conservatory to provide an extension to the house. It is 4.8 by 3 m (16 ft by 10 ft) and is very much used as a living area. It has been put up adjacent to the kitchen and is used a great deal for meals, as well as for entertaining, combining this with their barbeque on the patio.

To provide warmth in the winter Mr and Mrs Herbert are intending to extend the central heating into their conservatory, so even in cold weather they will be able to enjoy the pleasant view of the garden.

Mr and Mrs Herbert have certainly gone in for comfort. A floor has been constructed over the concrete base – chipboard supported on battens. This has been covered with carpet tiles. Curtains have been put up to give privacy in the evenings, and the conservatory is very well furnished with easy chairs and table, and even boasts a television.

Mr and Mrs Herbert are not intending to have many plants in their conservatory for they do not want to have too much moisture due to the floor covering. Nevertheless they are keen on plants but these are grown in a heated greenhouse.

Tony and Sheila Rees have an extremely picturesque garden and their Banbury California conservatory is enhanced by most attractive landscaping. The conservatory is used mainly as a living area. Many plants are grown outside in summer and taken into the conservatory for the winter; an orange tree is seen here in fruit.

Inside view of Mr and Mrs A. V. Herbert's Banbury Classic conservatory, also shown on p.13. It provides a spacious and, due to the translucent roof, 'light' extension to the house. The conservatory is used basically as a living area, proving especially useful on showery days when the barbeque is in use on the patio.

Modular designs

DICK AND TRICIA POWER
of Teddington Lock, Middlesex

The extensive roof terrace of Dick and Tricia Power's penthouse, which enjoys magnificent views of the river Thames, is laid out as a Japanese garden and incorporates a conservatory supplied by Alexander Bartholomew Conservatories Ltd. This timber conservatory has a pitched centre-ridged roof and a semi-hexagonal frontage, and is annexed to the south-west side of the apartment. It commands all-round visibility of the terrace, as well as a view of the river. The size is 4.8 by 3 m (16 by 10 ft).

The philosophy behind the positioning and orientation of the conservatory is pure Japanese in origin. It is based upon the principle of Shakkei, which means 'borrowed scenery' and is a technique for creating the illusion that a garden is larger than it really is. The idea is that since Dick and Tricia are lucky enough to have an attractive view from the terrace, they have incorporated this into the design of the garden itself, disguising its immediate boundaries, masking discordant elements and choosing plants compatible with the river and open-country scenery beyond.

Apart from the paramount objective of borrowing scenery and providing all-weather enjoyment of the roof terrace, the conservatory is much lived in. In sympathy with its immediate surroundings, it is furnished largely in the Japanese style, with Tatami mats, bare-board trim and surrounds, floor cushions and low table, and an overall emphasis on simplicity. It is, however, also used for overwintering less-hardy plants and for periodic display of Bonsai trees.

CHRIS ALBERT
of East Sheen, London

Mr Albert wishes this book had been published a couple of years ago when he was looking around for a suitable conservatory. He wanted something to blend in with his house, and found it in the end – a timber, half-octagonal ended conservatory from Alexander Bartholomew Conservatories Ltd. The size is 3.6 by 3 m (12 by 10 ft).

This conservatory is double glazed, faces east and is unheated, although Mr Albert will be extending the domestic central-heating system into it. However, the temperature did not drop below freezing during its first winter.

Access is from the kitchen and the conservatory is used a great deal for relaxing in, taking meals, etc.

This is a fairly recent acquisition and Mr Albert is still experimenting with plants – he is growing mainly houseplants including yuccas and begonias.

Tricia Power relaxes in her timber conservatory, supplied by Alexander Bartholomew Conservatories Ltd. The conservatory commands all-round visibility of the terrace roof garden and magnificent views over the river Thames.

(*Below*) After much searching for a conservatory which would blend in with his house, Chris Albert found this handsome, timber-framed, half-octagonal ended one, from Alexander Bartholomew Conservatories Ltd. The conservatory is double glazed and, perhaps because of this, the temperature did not drop below freezing during its first (unheated) winter.

MR AND MRS ADAM JOHNSTONE
of Capel, near Dorking, Surrey

Mr and Mrs Johnstone decided to invest in a spacious 4.8 by 4.5 m (16 by 15 ft) half-octagonal conservatory (made by Room Outside Ltd) because they are very keen on plants and also wanted extra space. Now the conservatory is used more than any other room, for relaxing in and for meals.

A minimum temperature of 13°C (55°F) is maintained (the central-heating system has been extended into the conservatory) which suits their range of plants, but the heating is turned up in the mornings to ensure a more comfortable living temperature. Shading and ventilation are automatic and cedar panelling on the dwarf walls helps to retain heat.

Mr and Mrs Johnstone love plants and among their pride and joy are standard fuchsias; *Phoenix canariensis*, a beautiful palm from the Canary Islands; philodendrons and sansevierias. Among other choice plants are aeoniums; alocasia; frangipani; bananas; oleander; strelitzia; citrus fruits of all kinds; setcreasia; mimosa; and the rare *Euphorbia capuronii*.

Mr and Mrs Johnstone have also raised shrubs and trees from seeds which they have collected in the West Indies.

Colour is provided by an assortment of pot plants, like the large-flowered tuberous begonias, the fibrous-rooted *Begonia semperflorens*, gloxinias, pelargoniums, lilies and cymbidium orchids.

The conservatory, adjoined on one side to a greenhouse in which plants are raised, is delightfully furnished with French garden furniture, and decorated with African masks.

Mr and Mrs Johnstone's conservatory contains a wealth of interesting plants, like a purple-leaved aeonium and a boldly veined anthurium. The flowers include begonias and gloxinias.

Mr and Mrs Adam Johnstone love plants and are able to grow a very wide range in their warm conservatory – many have been raised from seeds collected abroad. The tall purple-leaved plant is an aeonium, further colour being provided by such pot plants as begonias and gloxinias.

DAVID AND GILL CONS
of Roehampton, London

David and Jill Cons have invested in a modular timber conservatory from Room Outside Ltd which is used a great deal as a living area. Comfortably furnished, the floor has been laid with octagonal terra-cotta tiles, and a most attractive feature is the pool. It appears that the garden pool extends into the conservatory, but in fact there are two pools, separated by the conservatory wall. Fish in both add to the enjoyment of these features. This magnificent conservatory is 7.6 m (25ft) long, with a maximum width of about 3.6 m (12ft).

The conservatory is not heated but Mr and Mrs Cons grow a range of attractive plants. They started off with lots of ivies, but have progressed to oleander, lilies, impatiens, jasmine, etc.

They are tending, however, to go in more for evergreen foliage plants which give the conservatory a well-furnished look in winter. The large-leaved, hardy *Fatsia japonica* is proving very successful. A grape vine, planted with its roots outside the conservatory, provides lots of fruits in summer.

This view of the semi-octagonal end of David and Gill Cons' conservatory shows the very comfortable furniture and the flooring of terra-cotta tiles.

David and Gill Cons invested in this magnificent modular timber/brick conservatory from Room Outside Ltd. It is very comfortably furnished and the floor has been laid with octagonal terra-cotta tiles. The outside pool, shown also on p.31, is just to the right of the French windows. The conservatory 'atmosphere' is extended onto the terrace by careful choice of plants.

Custom-made designs

JOHN AND JILLY MATTHEWS
of Baxterley, Atherstone, Warwicks

This delightful and spacious Victorian-style conservatory recently tempted John and Jilly Matthews to buy the house. The conservatory was built by the previous owners of the house and won for them a Homemaker of the Year Competition. The length is 5.1 m (17 ft) and the width is 2.7 m (9 ft).

The conservatory is used as a living area all the year round, as the domestic central-heating has been extended into it, maintaining a very comfortable temperature.

The floor is tastefully covered with quarry tiles, and there is an abundance of space: for furniture like a three-seater settee and a hanging cane chair; and for plants such as a Passion flower, clematis, grape, ivy, etc. Hanging baskets add further interest and colour. John and Jilly like plenty of greenery and are gradually adding plants which appeal to them. They certainly have tremendous scope.

NORMAN AND TINA ELLIS
of Chislehurst, Kent

This tall L-shaped conservatory was designed and built by Norman and Tina Ellis and is built up to the first-floor level of the house. A first-floor window was converted into French doors, so there is access from two levels. The longer leg of the 'L' is approximately 7 × 2.4 m (23 × 8 ft) in area and the shorter one 5.1 × 3.0 m (17 ft × 10 ft).

The French doors give access to a cast-iron balcony (made from salvaged and renovated church radiator grilles). From the balcony a cast-iron spiral staircase (which was found half buried in a neighbour's garden) leads to the lower level of the conservatory.

Norman and Tina Ellis designed the timber section of the conservatory and bought a patent system of aluminium glazing bars for the roof, which is glazed with wire-reinforced glass. The floor is covered with white and black vinyl tiles laid direct onto the cement screed.

The Ellis' no longer own this conservatory, but when they did it was very much in use as a living area. It was not heated, but the central-heating boiler was installed there and the temperature did not go below zero. The conservatory is south-facing so was warmed by the sun.

Norman and Tina Ellis created plenty of colour with plants, like pelargoniums – some 2 m (6 ft) high – and with plumbago, bougainvillea, jasmine, and flowering annuals raised from seeds, like fragrant nicotiana. They even grew tomatoes, and had a productive grape vine trained into the roof, which still flourishes.

For photograph and drawing see pp.54 & 55

The Matthews' Victorian-style conservatory is extremely spacious and used all the year round, being heated by the domestic central-heating system. The floor is covered with quarry tiles. There is plenty of greenery, including aspidistras, grape ivy, ferns and a Passion flower on the wall.

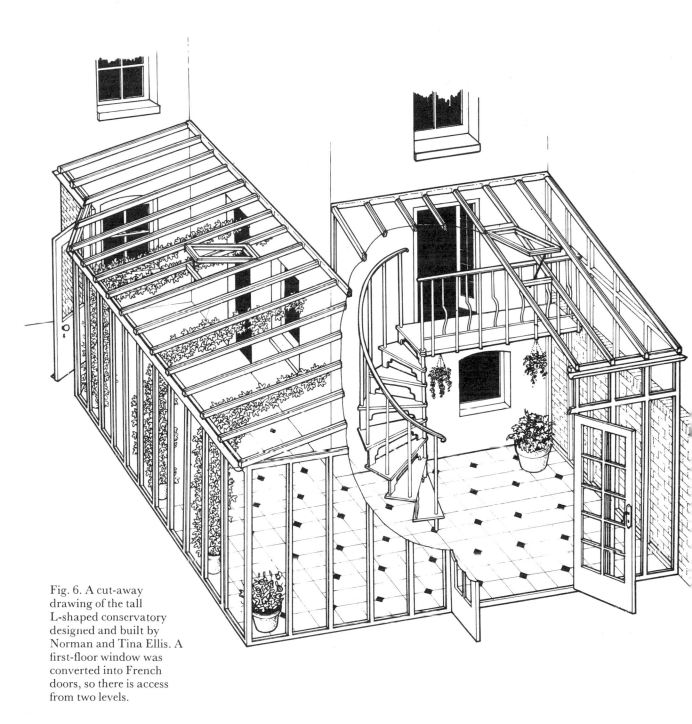

Fig. 6. A cut-away
drawing of the tall
L-shaped conservatory
designed and built by
Norman and Tina Ellis. A
first-floor window was
converted into French
doors, so there is access
from two levels.

(*Opposite*) This tall L-shaped conservatory was designed and built by Norman and Tina
Ellis, and extends to the first-floor level of the house. The balcony was made from
salvaged and renovated church radiator grilles and the cast-iron staircase was found in a
neighbour's garden. The construction is timber, with aluminium glazing bars for the
roof.

DENIS AND AUDREY HAYES
of Surbiton, Surrey

Denis and Audrey Hayes have always wanted a greenhouse or conservatory and were delighted when, seven years ago, they found a house with a very large conservatory attached.

It is Edwardian and appears to be custom-built, constructed of timber and cast-iron on 1 m (3 ft) high brick walls. It is about 6 by 4.2 m (20 by 14 ft) and 4.5 m (15 ft) high. Entry is from the sitting room and it has two other doors, and opening side windows, so there is adequate provision for ventilation.

The conservatory is kept frost-free over the winter by means of a fan heater, and some of the more tender plants are taken indoors at the onset of cold weather.

When Mr and Mrs Hayes first moved into their house the conservatory was full of pelargoniums, heavily infested with whitefly, but this problem is now under control. Several large and old cacti have been kept, but Mr and Mrs Hayes are still experimenting with plants. They are now growing such plants as lilies, cannas, plumbago, bougainvillea and trailing fuchsias.

The conservatory is tiled with a herringbone pattern of quarry tiles and there are soil beds on each side which have now been covered with a horticultural aggregate and are used for standing pot plants. There is also a little pool with rocks around it. Mr and Mrs Hayes have furnished their conservatory with a white table and chairs and find it a delightful setting for occasional entertaining.

There are many fascinating plants in Denis and Audrey Hayes' conservatory, like cannas (with large orange flowers), cacti and other succulent plants, shown here clustered around the rock pool.

This magnificent Edwardian conservatory, belonging to Denis and Audrey Hayes, evokes all the grandeur of that era. The conservatory, constructed *c.* 1905, is brick built to a height of 1m (3 ft), with glass and timber frame above, and with period cast-iron supports for the roof. It is 6 m (20 ft) long with a door at the end communicating to the lounge (*right*). The width is 4.2 m (14 ft) and there are side doors leading to front (*foreground*) and rear gardens. The height to the apex is 4.5 m (15 ft). Note that the sloping roof glazing is at two levels, allowing the incorporation of 'vertical' ventilation windows in the glazing between them.

THE RIGHT HONOURABLE NORMAN ST JOHN-STEVAS
of Knightsbridge, London

While Victorian styles of conservatory are popular today, especially with city and town dwellers, the Gothic style is also becoming more widely used. This was chosen by The Right Honourable Norman St John-Stevas to create an illusion of space in his tall and narrow London home. He has successfully transformed the first floor of his home into a spacious and light conservatory filled with plants.

'The purpose of my conservatory', said Mr St John-Stevas, 'is to enjoy the benefit of plants all the year round. In theory one could sit in it – in practice I do not'.

However, this delightful conservatory is heated by means of its own central-heating system. His favourite plants flourish here, and the spring sees camellias and azaleas in flower, together with mimosa.

In the summer the bougainvillea is in full bloom, together with plumbago and 'geraniums' or pelargoniums. A grape vine produces bunches of fruits. A rather unusual subject (at least in this country) is an olive tree.

The plants are grown in large clay pots and other attractive containers, most of which are placed on the beautiful black and white marble floor which was laid in a diamond pattern. Water also features in this conservatory, in the form of a fountain. The sound of moving water is very soothing and what better place to enjoy it than in a conservatory?

Mr St John-Stevas explained that the wooden traceries on the windows are 13th Century Gothic French perpendicular in design. These detach for cleaning which, to my mind, is an extremely good idea.

The spacious conservatory is in two parts, the first part being 4 m (13 ft) long and 2.7 m (9 ft) wide and the second part being 3 m (10 ft) long and 2 m (6½ ft) wide.

The Right Honourable Norman St John-Stevas wanted to create an impression of space in his tall and narrow city house and has achieved this with a beautiful Gothic-style conservatory. Here plants are enjoyed all the year round, including azaleas, camellias, bougainvillea, mimosa and geraniums. He also has a grape vine and an olive tree. The conservatory has a black and white marble floor, a fountain and its own central-heating system.

ANTHONY AND ALYSON HUXLEY
of Surbiton, Surrey

When Anthony and Alyson Huxley were looking for a house ten years ago they agreed that they either wanted one with a conservatory or at least a place to erect one. No good conservatories showed up, but they did end up with a site, a paved area beyond the French windows of the sitting room and kitchen which open at the back of the house, with the garden beyond. The position faces east, but gets sun from dawn till at least 2 p.m. in the summer, and even this restricted amount of sun can raise the temperature enormously in summer.

An intermediate roof between ground and first-floor windows unfortunately restricted the upper roof level to 2.5 m (8½ ft). Also, on one side, a steep-sloping annexe housing an oil tank had to form one side wall. These constraints knocked out several ready-made possibilities. The Huxleys did not want to invest in a Victorian-style special design then beginning to be offered, so consulted Alitex Ltd, who came up with an ingenious combination of their lean-to and orthodox peaked aluminium designs, giving sloped side areas down to 1.5 m (5 ft) and the full 2.5 m (8½ ft) headroom in the centre.

To soften the relative starkness of the structure, Anthony added 'Victoriana' in the shape of a strip cut from some otherwise horrid low plastic fencing panels and used another part of the moulding inside. 'It is almost convincing!', he said.

Originally the structure, some 5.1 m (17 ft) wide across the house wall, was 2.8 m (9½ ft) deep. After a couple of years it became clear that more space was needed so another section was added, making the total depth 4.2 m (14 ft).

Because the original dwarf support walls and aluminium struts could not be removed, this gave rise to two 'annexes' on each side of the central double door into the garden. Anthony made deep two-tier wooden staging for each, having previously made a tall, staggered, three-tier stage, 76 cm (30 in) at its widest, on one side. Apart from the staging, a three-tiered Victorian jardinière holds small flowering plants.

Heat is provided by two electric fan heaters, thermostatically controlled to give a maximum of 10°C (50°F) in winter; on really cold nights they may not provide more than about 7°C (45°F). Originally natural-gas heaters were installed but the fumes from these proved lethal to many plants. 'These heaters may be fine for keeping conservatories frost-free', said Anthony, 'but at higher temperatures they pump too many fumes into the air – and in winter providing adequate ventilation meant that too much heat was being allowed to escape.'

Ventilation is provided by four 60 cm (2 ft) square automatic vents and two 60 cm by 1.2 m (2 by 4 ft) manually operated ones.

The floor is entirely covered in hexagonal paving slabs, but this has proved to be a slight mistake. Some direct planting positions would have paid off in allowing climbers to develop properly: it has been found that few enjoy root restriction. Two plants which have rooted through their pots and between paving cracks – a plumbago and an ivy-leaf

(*Above*) This conservatory, belonging to Anthony and Alyson Huxley, was supplied by Alitex Ltd., and is an ingenious combination of their lean-to and orthodox peaked aluminium designs. Anthony Huxley added the 'Victorian' roof mouldings. The conservatory is 5.1 m (17 ft) wide and 4.2 m (14 ft) deep.

Anthony and Alyson Huxley enjoying some refreshment in their plant-filled conservatory. Here can be seen the beautiful purple tibouchina, pelargoniums, yellow abutilon, fuchsias, and the large-leaved *Fatsia japonica*.

pelargonium – have shown what can be achieved and so Anthony plans to open up a few planting holes.

Summer shading is given to the glass only on the sunward walls and the first 60 cm (2 ft) row of roof panes; more would be desirable, but in the absence of slotted roof bars it is impossible to fix internal shading properly. Anthony and Alyson are trying to find a heavy-foliaged climber, maybe a Passion flower, to provide shade in summer and also to conceal partially the rather stark internal aluminium struts.

The Huxleys consider a conservatory should undoubtedly be a place for displaying plants rather than for growing them on. They get the best of both worlds by using the 'annexes' for seedlings, cuttings and plants coming on, but even so they have differences over the inhabitants. Alyson would like relatively few large, bold plants, but Anthony cannot resist a large variety and so there are (still) a lot of oddities in smallish pots, especially on the staging. In winter the problem is made worse because tender plants from the garden, mainly pelargoniums and fuchsias, need shelter. Some lurk in a cold utility greenhouse at the far end of the garden, but the best have to come into the conservatory.

Since large plants are permanent they have to be attractive in leaf as well as in any flower. Big specimens in present residence include: *Acacia baileyana*, mimosa, which flowers in mid-winter; *Araucaria excelsa*, the Norfolk Island pine, becoming too spreading; a 2 m (6 ft) tall form of *Cyperus alternifolius* and its relation the papyrus; *Dracaena draco*, the dragon tree, grown from seed and after 20 years reaching a height of 1.5 m (5 ft) in a 45 cm (18 in) pot; *Hedychium gardnerianum* with lovely fragrant flowers and handsome leaves; some oleanders; a fremontodendron, which is kept cut back; *Brachychiton populneus* with thin acer-like leaves; and tibouchina with splendid purple flowers.

Medium-sized plants include: *Acacia armata*, which will get big; *Prostanthera sieberi*, the Australian mint-bush with lovely mauve winter flowers; the lemon-scented *Pelargonium* 'Mabel Grey'; plumbagos, which are kept bushy; variegated *Pittosporum tobira;* flowering and variegated abutilons; *Hibiscus rosa-sinensis* and variety *cooperi,* the latter with white foliage; some bromeliads; strelitzia; bush-grown bougainvilleas, which would be better if allowed to climb; *Datura sanguinea* and *D. knightii;* and *Breynia nivosa,* a marvellous effect of white, green and red on neat foliage.

There are many ferns including a tree fern now nine years old with a 15 cm (6 in) trunk and 1.2 m (4 ft) leaf-span, and the neat palm-like *Blechnum gibbum*; wide-spreading woodwardia; and stagshorn ferns, *Platycerium alcicorne* and *P. grande,* both esconced on tubes of cork bark and getting impressively large.

Colour comes from pelargoniums in small pots, a few fuchsias, begonias, achimenes and streptocarpus, and from red-leaved iresine and purple-leaved strobilanthes. Baskets liven up the roof, and contain mainly setcreasea, tradescantia and zebrina; and *Kalanchoë manginii* and the silver-leaved *K. pumila* for winter flowers.

Four spot-lights, two high and two low, allow the conservatory to be admired at night.

Watering is carried out by hose in summer but has to be done by can in winter – which the Huxleys find very tedious – because the mains water is too cold; another argument for less plants.

Feeding and repotting are also done less frequently than they should be because of shortage of time – Anthony feels that plants like abutilons look tatty as a result. He uses a peat-based compost for the smaller plants, with slow-release fertilizer and some vermiculite added. The bigger plants go into a John Innes plus peat-based compost mix (the latter because Anthony finds the modern John Innes compost always seems extremely heavy and soggy). He feels that much more feeding would pay off but, as already noted, it does get put aside.

Pests which are a problem are whitefly, especially on fuchsias and pelargoniums, mealy bug (on plumbago) and scale insects (on oleander, ferns, etc). Spraying is carried out when needed.

MR AND MRS J. van ZWANENBERG
of Woking, Surrey

Mr and Mrs van Zwanenberg have a Roman-style house with a truly magnificent 12 m (40 ft) square atrium containing a wealth of interesting plant collected from all over the world.

The atrium is a covered courtyard with all the rooms of the house opening into it. It even has Roman-style underfloor heating (although, of course, in a modern version), maintaining a minimum temperature of 15.5°C (60°F). The domed roof is double glazed, with a central funnel to draw out hot air, which creates an insulating layer of hot air in the roof.

The plants are sprayed twice daily by means of overhead sprinklers, using rainwater from a tank in the roof. The walking area around the edge of the central plant area is tiled with blue and white Florentine tiles. A delightful feature is the lily pool and waterfall, containing blue waterlilies.

The range of plants grown reads like a nurseryman's catalogue, and includes a hoya trained around the roof, and a *Ficus pumila* completely covering one wall. Strelitzias flower twice a year and jasmine scents the atrium in winter. Other climbers include bougainvilleas, lapageria, stephanotis, plumbago and streptosolen.

Seasonal colour is also provided by shrubs like hibiscus, *Abutilon* 'Golden Fleece' and *A. megapotamicum*, callistemon, nerium and clerodendron; and by perennials such as anthuriums and crossandra.

There are many luxuriant foliage plants, including ferns, bromeliads, calathea, codiaeums, diffenbachia, cordyline, dracaena, monstera, philodendrons, ctenanthe, maranta, ficus, fittonia and palms. Truly a plantsman's paradise.

For photograph see over:

Breathtaking in its size, this 12 m (40 ft) square atrium, or covered courtyard, belonging to Mr and Mrs J. van Zwanenberg, contains a wealth of tropical and sub-tropical plants, which thrive in the warm humid environment. Seen here are such plants as variegated pineapple, red anthuriums in flower, and aeschynanthus in a hanging basket. The plants' needs are well catered for with underfloor heating, overhead sprinklers and a central funnel to draw out hot air.

6

PLANTS FOR ALL SEASONS

There is a wealth of plants available for growing in the conservatory, from those which can take very cool conditions to flamboyant tropical kinds. Of course, they should be chosen to suit the minimum temperature you are able to maintain; but whatever this minimum may be, you can be assured there are sufficient plants to provide colour and interest all the year round.

Many people will not be able to provide sufficient heat to keep tropical plants flourishing during the atumn, winter and early spring. Nevertheless, such plants can be displayed in the conservatory during the warmer summer months, and indeed they will greatly benefit from a spell under glass. For the rest of the year they can be kept in a warm room indoors and treated as houseplants.

The following descriptive lists contain some of the most popular plants for growing in conservatories. The shrubs and climbers will provide a permanent 'framework' to the planting scheme, especially if planted in beds and borders, while pot plants can be used among them for colour all through the year, together with plants which grow from bulbs, corms and tubers.

To my mind, plenty of foliage pants should be used, too, to provide a lush 'jungle' atmosphere, and to act as a foil to brightly coloured flowers.

Pools are becoming popular features in many conservatories and really they are no more difficult to manage than an outdoor pool. Tender aquatic plants, including tropical waterlilies, are easier to grow than you might imagine and therefore I make no apologies for including aquatic plants in my lists.

And finally do not forget fruits: I have included the traditional conservatory kinds: grapes, peaches and nectarines, and the citrus fruits.

It is becoming very much easier to buy the more exotic plants, due, I think, to public demand. The larger garden centres, and even well-known chain-stores, now carry a wide range of tender plants, including less-common genera and species. This is due to the fact that producers of greenhouse plants and houseplants are obtaining, propagating and distributing some of the more unusual plants.

Temperatures

The lists contain all the basic cultural information you are likely to need. Do bear in mind that the temperature quoted for each plant is the **minimum** acceptable temperature. Most plants will enjoy higher temperatures than these by day and during the summer.

Shrubs

ABUTILON

Temperature: 10°C (50°F).

Characteristics: The abutilons are easily grown shrubs and some of the taller-growing kinds are amenable to training on walls, pillars, etc. Most are grown for their attractive bell-shaped flowers produced in summer, but do consider also those with colourful variegated foliage. Most have fairly large leaves, rather maple-like in shape. For flowers I can recommend several of the hybrids, particularly 'Ashford Red', which is crimson; the beautiful yellow 'Canary Bird' or 'Golden Fleece'; and the red-orange 'Firebell'. For variegated foliage, one of the most striking is the hybrid 'Savitzii', with white and green leaves. Unlike the other hybrids, which grown up to 1.8 m (6 ft), this one is a low grower and makes a fine pot specimen. Tall, and suitable for training, is A. *striatum* 'Thompsonii' which has striking yellow-mottled leaves.

Cultivation: Any well-drained soil is suitable, and if pot grown I prefer to use soil-based compost. Water and feed plants well in summer and provide an airy atmosphere. To prevent leggy growth plants are best pruned hard back in early spring each year. Easily propagated from cuttings in summer.

ACACIA   Wattle

Temperature: 10°C (50°F), or slightly lower.

Characteristics: The wattles are evergreen shrubs or trees, many of them quite tall. The foliage is attractive and masses of small, powder-puff-like flowers appear in spring. Most easily available are the Cootamunda wattle, A. *baileyana*, with bluish-grey foliage, and the silver wattle, A. *dealbata*, with silvery foliage (this is one you see in florists' shops).

Cultivation: Good drainage is needed, plus maximum light and plenty of ventilation (in winter as well if the weather is mild). Water well in summer but keep only slightly moist in winter. Routine pruning is not required but as the plants grow tall you will need to cut them back when they reach the roof and this is best done immediately flowering is over. I find wattles are best grown against a wall of the conservatory to prevent them spreading too much.

APHELANDRA   Zebra plant

Temperature: 10°C (50°F), but a little higher if possible.

Characteristics: There are several species of these evergreen shrubs but the one usually grown is A. *squarrosa* 'Louisae', popularly known as the zebra plant because its large green leaves are boldly striped with white. It has a remarkable flower head, consisting of bright yellow bracts (modified leaves) in the shape of a pyramid, through which poke small flowers.

Cultivation: Plants are generally pot grown but there is no reason why they should not be planted in a bed if you can maintain the minimum temperature. Shade from strong sun should be provided in spring and summer and, when temperatures are high, provide high atmospheric humidity. Liquid feeding in summer is also beneficial. After a time plants are inclined to become leggy, so to prevent this happening cut back the stems after flowering, by about one-third to half, when new growth from lower down will be produced, giving a bushy specimen.

BOUVARDIA

Temperature: 10°C (50°F).

Characteristics: These are small evergreen shrubs, ideal for limited space. Those usually grown are cultivars of B. × *domestica*, and they bloom over a very long period in the summer and into autumn. Try to obtain the cultivar 'President Cleveland' which has scarlet flowers, or the rose-pink 'Rosea'.

Cultivation: Grow in a well-drained soil bed or in pots of soil-based compost. Good ventilation is needed in the growing season, plus light shade from strong sun. Water freely in spring and summer, but during autumn and winter keep the plants only slightly moist. It is best to pinch out the growing tips of young plants several times to create bushy specimens. Plants should be pruned in early spring by cutting back to one bud all shoots produced in the previous year. Do not hang on to old plants, but replace them regularly with young ones – soft cuttings can be rooted in spring in a heated propagating case.

BRUNFELSIA

Temperature: 10°C (50°F).

Characteristics: These are spectacular but easy evergreen shrubs which are suited to the small conservatory and they bloom over a long period in the summer. The best-known species is *B. calycina* with scented, fairly large blue-purple flowers. There are several varieties of this which are well worth searching for, including *B. c. floribunda* which has darker flowers, and *B. c. macrantha* which is noted for its larger blooms. I am also particularly fond of the species *B. latifolia* with scented blooms of a pale violet shade, and *B. undulata* which has fragrant white blooms, attractively waved at the edges.

Cultivation: Best grown in a soil bed, but happy in a large pot or tub in well-drained soil-based compost. I pinch out the growing tips of young plants to ensure bushy, well-branched specimens. General cultivation is simple enough: shade from strong sun, water as required in the growing season, plus occasional liquid feeds, with less water in autumn and winter. Established plants do not need pruning.

CALLISTEMON   Bottle brush

Temperature: 4.5°C (40°F).

Characteristics: Ideal shrubs for the small cool conservatory, producing in summer unusual flowers, which do indeed look like a bottle brush. They are Australian shrubs, with evergreen foliage, and the blooms are generally in shades of red. The flowers consist mainly of long stamens and it is these which form the 'brush'. Buy whichever species you find on offer: it could be *C. citrinus*, *C. linearis*, *C. rigidus*, *C. speciosus* or *C. subulatus*. Each one is well worth growing.

Cultivation: Callistemons can be grown in a soil bed or in pots, and drainage must be very good, soil-based compost being recommended for pot culture. Soil or compost must be acid or lime-free. As with most Australian shrubs, provide plenty of ventilation and ensure plants receive a good quantity of sunshine. If plants are pot grown, stand them out of doors for the summer in a sunny sheltered spot. This will help to ripen the new shoots.

CAMELLIA

Temperature: 4.5–10°C (40–50°F); also unheated conservatory.

Characteristics: These evergreen shrubs have shiny dark green foliage which makes a superb background for the red, pink or white flowers which are produced in winter or spring. Camellias are hardy and can also be grown out of doors. I recommend cultivars of *C. japonica*. An excellent modern variety especially recommended for the conservatory, where its fragrance will be noticeable, is 'Scentsation', which has pink flowers. Also try some of the *C. reticulata* and *C. × williamsii* cultivars: highly popular is *C. × williamsii* 'Donation' with pink flowers.

Cultivation: I think in the amateur conservatory plants are best grown in pots, potting them on until eventually they are in tubs. It is essential to use an acid or lime-free compost. I make up a mix consisting of mainly peat and leafmould, but add a little coarse sand and acid loam. If you do not want to go to this trouble, buy a proprietary ericaceous compost from a garden centre. The plants are taken under glass in the autumn; provide really good ventilation and make sure the compost does not dry out. It should be kept steadily moist but not wet.

When flowering is over stand the plants outside in a sheltered, semi-shaded spot. Ideally plunge the pots in weathered ashes so that the compost does not dry out rapidly.

A warm conservatory is a haven for sumptuous tropical plants, like the yellow-flowered *Aphelandra squarrosa* 'Louisae', and foliage plants like coloured-leaved codiaeums and green-leaved aglaeonemas.

Keep the compost steadily moist throughout the growing season. In the summer plants will benefit from liquid feeding every two weeks. Try to use rainwater for watering if you have 'hard' tapwater.

CASSIA

Temperature: 4.5°C (40°F).
Characteristics: These shrubs are in the pea family and the species usually grown is *C. corymbosa*. This is evergreen and grows to about 2 m (6 ft) tall. In summer and autumn there is a good display of deep yellow blooms. An ideal plant for the small cool conservatory.
Cultivation: Grow in pots or soil bed, making sure drainage is good. Use soil-based potting compost. The plants will benefit from being stood out of doors for the summer, choosing a sunny spot. Water well in spring and summer, but far less in autumn and winter, when the compost or soil should be kept only just moist. Prune the plants in late winter by cutting back to within 5 cm (2 in) all shoots produced in the previous year.

CESTRUM

Temperature: 7–10°C (45–50°F).
Characteristics: These are fairly tall evergreen or semi-evergreen shrubs but nevertheless are suitable for the smallish conservatory if they are grown against a wall or pillar, to stop the stems from spreading outwards. They are grown for their clusters of tubular flowers which appear in summer and autumn. There are several species which are fairly easily obtainable, including the bright orange *C. aurantiacum*, 3 m (10 ft); the red-purple *C. elegans* 3 m; the crimson *C. 'Newellii'*, 2 m (6 ft); and the bright pink *C. roseum*, also 2 m.
Cultivation: Grow in a soil bed if possible, or failing that a large pot or tub. The growing medium should be high in humus so add plenty of peat to the soil or use a peat-based potting compost. The plants will take plenty of water in the growing season, but ease up in autumn and winter. Feed regularly in sum-

mer and provide shade from strong sun. Train the stems to a system of horizontal wires, and allow if desired the stems to grow into the roof area. In late winter carry out pruning: remove all three-year-old stems, and prune out the old flowered tops of those remaining.

CROSSANDRA

Temperature: 15.5°C (60°F).
Characteristics: The crossandras are tropical evergreen shrubs of modest size, suitable for pot culture in a small conservatory. The species usually available is *C. infundibuliformis* with flamboyant orange-red blooms in the summer on stems up to about 91 cm (3 ft) in height.
Cultivation: In warm conditions provide high humidity and light shading from strong sun. Water normally in the spring and summer, but keep only just moist in autumn and winter. Feed fortnightly in summer. To prevent leggy growth prune back the stems by about half in early spring.

DATURA   Angel's trumpets

Temperature: 10°C (50°F), or little lower.
Characteristics: large, vigorous, evergreen or deciduous shrubs with huge trumpet-shaped blooms in the summer and autumn – hence the common name. They are more suitable for the larger conservatory. Several species which you may come across in garden centres include *D. cornigera* with scented white or cream flowers, 3 m (10 ft); *D. c. 'Knightii'*, a double-flowered form in the same colour; the superb orange-red *D. sanguinea*, 2 m (6 ft); and the well-scented white *D. suaveolens*, a giant at 5 m (16 ft).
Cultivation: Daturas are best grown in a soil border due to their vigour, but I have had good results with large pots or tubs. In the summer a good deal of ventilation should be provided with light shade from strong sunshine. Despite the fact they are vigorous, the plants benefit from regular feeding during the summer about once a fortnight – with liquid fertilizer. Most people will need to

restrict the height of these shrubs and this can be done by cutting back last year's stems to within 15 cm (6 in) of ground level in late winter.

ERYTHRINA Coral tree

Temperature: 4.5°C (40°F).
Characteristics: This is one of my great favourites for it has flamboyant flowers in summer, and despite the fact that it is a native of Brazil, it is almost hardy and easily grown. The species grown is *E. crista-galli* (the specific name meaning cock's comb), which produces scarlet pea-like flowers. The leaves are trifoliate and carried on spiny stems which grow to about 2 m (6 ft) in height.
Cultivation: In the spring and summer make sure the plant has really good light and ventilation. Water as required in the growing season, but in winter the soil or compost should be kept virtually dry as the plant will be resting. The leaves fall in the autumn. In spring cut back all stems to within a few centimetres of the soil. New stems will then be produced. Grow in a large pot or tub, or in a soil border. Drainage must be good. I raised my plants from seeds sown in heat in spring and they made terrific growth during the first season.

GARDENIA Cape jasmine

Temperature: 15.5°C (60°F).
Characteristics: *Gardenia jasminoides* is an evergreen shrub from China which produces beautifully scented white flowers in summer and autumn. The height is around 2 m (6 ft) when given the freedom of a soil bed or border, but much less when grown in a pot.
Cultivation: I find that plants grow well in peat-based composts. In the summer high humidity is needed, together with shade from strong sun. Feed with a liquid fertilizer once a fortnight. I pinch out the tips of young plants to create really bushy specimens, and immediately after flowering I cut back the stems by about half.

HIBISCUS Shrubby mallow

Temperature: 10°C (50°F).
Characteristics: The speci   usually grown is *H. rosa-sinensis*, which is a very common sight in hotel gardens in the Mediterranean countries. The plant orginates from China, though. It is a deciduous shrub with large, flared, deep-red flowers in summer. Height is about 2 m (6 ft). In recent years many cultivars have come on the market whose colours include red, pink, yellow, orange and white. An old cultivar is *H. rosa-sinensis* 'Cooperi' whose leaves are variegated white and green. The flowers are red.

I think foreign holidays have resulted in hibiscus becoming very popular in recent years, as they are a common sight in Mediterranean countries, particularly in the gardens of tourist hotels.
Cultivation: I prefer to grow hibiscus in a soil bed, but good results are possible in large pots or tubs. Use a well-drained soil-based compost when potting. Only light shade from strong sun is needed in summer, but high humidity is desirable. Water well in summer, and feed regularly, but keep only slightly moist in winter. In late winter plants can be pruned fairly hard to keep them small.

JACOBINIA

Temperature: 13°C (55°F).
Characteristics: The jacobinias are evergreen shrubs from Brazil and flower in the summer, being ideal subjects for the small conservatory. The two species most easily obtainable are *J. carnea* with bright pink flowers carried in dense spikes, to a height of 2 m (6 ft), and the 60 cm (2 ft) tall *J. pauciflora* with scarlet blooms in clusters.
Cultivation: Ideal subjects for pots, using a soil based compost. In the summer water normally and give liquid feeds about once a fortnight. Also give light shade and provide a humid atmosphere. Keep the compost on the dry side during the autumn and winter. I prune plants after flowering each year by cutting back the stems really hard – to within 5 cm (2 in) of the compost surface.

LANTANA

Temperature: 7°C (45°F).

Characteristics: *Lantana camara* is a small shrub from the West Indies and has become naturalized throughout the tropics. It's ideal for the small conservatory, bearing a long succession of yellow flowers in summer and autumn. There are several cultivars which may have yellow, pink, red or white blooms.

Cultivation: If grown in a soil bed it will make quite a wide-spreading bush, but it is also suitable for pot cultivation. Ensure well-drained soil or compost. A good deal of sunshine is needed plus plenty of ventilation in the summer. Keep only slightly moist during the autumn and winter. I prefer to replace plants frequently with young specimens, which are more compact. Cuttings taken in spring or early summer are easily rooted in a heated propagating case. Pinch out the tips of young plants to create bushy specimens. In early spring older plants can be cut back to within 15 cm (6 in) of compost level.

NERIUM   Oleander

Temperature: 7°C (45°F).

Characteristics: *Nerium oleander* is a familiar sight in Mediterranean gardens, from where it originates. It is an evergreen shrub to about 2 m (6 ft) in height and in summer and autumn bears pink, red or purple-red blooms. Look out, too, for cultivars, such as the double white 'Album Plenum', the double pink 'Roseum Plenum', and 'Variegatum', whose leaves are edged with cream.

Cultivation: Basic conditions to provide are good ventilation and plenty of sun. I find that plants benefit from a spell out of doors in the summer, taking them inside again during September. Carry out watering as necessary in the spring and summer, but in autumn and winter keep the soil or compost on the dry side. Appy liquid fertilizer fortnightly in summer. I prefer to grow plants in pots, eventually moving them to large pots or tubs. Use soil-based compost.

RHODODENDRON

Temperature: 7°C (45°F).

Characteristics: The tender rhododendrons are ideal subjects for the cool conservatory. The most popular is the so-called Indian azalea, cultivars of *R. simsii*, which bloom in the autumn and winter. At that period garden centres and florists' shops are full of these azaleas, which come in various colours – shades or pink, red, white, etc. Cultivars of the similar *R. indicum* are also available. Both types are low-growing evergreens. More difficult to obtain are several other tender rhododendrons, such as *R. lindleyi* with highly fragrant white waxy blooms. This is a large shrub, growing to about 3 m (10 ft) in height.

Cultivation: Soil or compost for rhododendrons must be acid or lime-free. They can be grown in a soil bed, but are more generally pot grown. Use an ericaceous compost, or mix your own: equal parts by volume of peat and leafmould, plus some coarse sand and a little base fertilizer. Water regularly throughout the year as the soil or compost must not be allowed to dry out. In summer apply liquid fertilizer once a fortnight, plenty of ventilation, moderate humidity, and light shade from strong sun.

SPARMANNIA   African hemp

Temperature: 7°C (45°F).

Characteristics: *Sparmannia africana* is an evergreen shrub from South Africa, suited to the cool conservatory. It has large heart-shaped leaves and white blooms in spring and summer.

Cultivation: When grown in a soil border it makes a large specimen, 2.4 m (8 ft) in height and spread. It might be better, therefore, to grow it in a large pot to restrict its size. Use well-drained soil-based compost. In the summer water normally, but keep only slightly moist in the autumn and winter. In the growing season feed about once a fortnight, and ensure plenty of ventilation and light shade from strong sun.

Here a pergola has been constructed to support *Bougainvillea* 'Miss Manila Hybrid'.

TIBOUCHINA Glory bush

Temperature: 10°C (50°F).

Characteristics: *Tibouchina semidecandra*, the species generally grown, is an evergreen shrub from Brazil, attaining about 3 m (10 ft) in height. It has attractive velvety leaves, and in summer and autumn produces beautiful blue-purple, saucer-shaped blooms.

Cultivation: Grow in a soil border or in pots of soil-based potting compost. Water normally in spring and summer, but keep only just moist in winter. Liquid feed once a fortnight when in full growth and provide light shade. To keep the plant on the small side, when it can be grown in limited space, prune the stems hard back in winter. If you do not wish to restrict size, tibouchina makes a good wall shrub – train it up the back wall of the conservatory and even up into the roof. Pot-grown plants will need to have their stems supported with thin bamboo canes.

Climbers

ALLAMANDA

Temperature: 15.5°C (60°F).

Characteristics: *Allamanda cathartica* is a sumptuous evergreen climber from South America. Being of tropical origin it needs warm conditions. When happy it grows vigorously, producing in summer and autumn large trumpet-shaped flowers in bright yellow. There are two varieties which you may come across: 'Grandiflora' with pale yellow blooms and 'Hendersonii' which is deep golden-yellow.

Cultivation: It can be grown in a soil border but is also suitable for a large pot, using soil based compost. In summer, shade from strong sunshine and ensure high humidity. The stems should be trained to supports and be well spaced out. Allamanda should be pruned in early spring each year by cutting back the growth made in the previous season to within two buds of its base.

The allamanda has a milky sap which can cause irritation if it comes in contact with eyes or mouth.

BOUGAINVILLEA Paper flower

Temperature: 10°C (50°F).

Characteristics: This vigorous Brazilian climber is one of the most popular conservatory plants and despite its flamboyant appearance is easily grown. The flowers are insignificant: it is the highly colourful paper-like bracts that surround them which create the display in summer. Two species are generally available: *B. glabra*, widely planted in Mediterranean countries, with purple bracts, and *B. spectabilis*, with reddish or purple bracts. In recent years many hybrids have become available like the orange 'Golden Glow'; 'Mrs Butt', crimson to magenta; 'Brilliant', copper-orange; and 'Orange King', with orange bracts.

Cultivation: Ideal for large-pot cultivation, using a well-drained soil-based compost, or for a soil bed. If you do not have much space grow it in a pot and train it to a framework of canes – the stems can be looped to keep them within bounds. Carry out regular pruning in early spring by removing all weak or spindly shoots. The strong remaining stems can then be cut back by at least one-third if necessary. Bougainvilleas need plenty of sunshine, good ventilation and high humidity in summer. In winter, keep the soil/compost on the dry side and increase watering as growth commences in the spring.

CLERODENDRON

Temperature: 15.5°C (60°F).

Characteristics: The West African *C. thomsonae*, the species normally grown in conservatories, is an evergreen climber which attains about 4 m (13 ft) in height. It flowers in the summer, when it carries striking crimson flowers surrounded by a white calyx.

Cultivation: Easily grown, it also makes a good house plant in winter if pot grown, for it does need a high minimum winter temperature. Grow in a well-drained soil bed or large pot of soil-based compost. Space out the stems and tie them in to suitable supports as they grow. No regular pruning is needed but if desired side shoots can be shortened by up to half in early spring. Any weak or straggly shoots can also be removed. In summer, water well, give good ventilation and lightly shade from strong sun. In autumn and winter keep the compost/soil only just moist. Feed once a fortnight in the summer, using a weak liquid fertilizer.

CLIANTHUS Parrot's bill

Temperature: 7–10°C (45–50°F).
Characteristics: These climbers, which are in the pea family, come from Australia and New Zealand and are ideal for the cool conservatory. The pinnate foliage is attractive and the large pea-like blooms in spring or summer will be the envy of your visitors. *C. puniceus* is the species usually grown. It attains a modest 2 m (6 ft) in height and has red flowers. There is also a white form of this called 'Albus'.
Cultivation: Grow the parrot's bill in a border or large pot, ensuring drainage is very good. Use a soil-based compost for pot culture and put plenty of drainage material in the bottom. Very good light is needed but a little shade from the strongest sun will be appreciated. Water normally when in full growth but be sparing in winter.

DIPLADENIA Pink allamanda

Temperature: 15.5°C (60°F).
Characteristics: The dipladenias are evergreen climbers from tropical America with sumptuous trumpet-like flowers which appear mainly in the summer. There are several species but the one generally available is *D. splendens* (also known as *Mandevilla splendens*). Growing up to 3 m (10 ft) or more in height, it bears rose-pink flowers over a long period and has evergreen foliage.
Cultivation: Well-drained conditions are essential. Grow in a soil border or in a large pot of soil-based potting compost. If pot grown, twine the stems around a system of bamboo canes. If you wish to keep the plant within bounds, cut it back hard after flowering. All the growths produced in the past growing season can be pruned to within 5 cm (2 in) of their base. However, if you want the plant to fill a lot of space, then prune less severely or leave well alone. In summer ensure high humidity and light shade, and water normally. In winter, water only as the compost is starting to dry out.

HOYA Wax flower

Temperature: 7°C (45°F).
Characteristics: *Hoya carnosa*, a native of Queensland, is one of the most popular climbers for the conservatory and ideally suited to the smaller structure. It is evergreen, having rather thick fleshy leaves, and is rather a slow grower. Pendulous clusters of white waxy flowers, which turn pinkish as they age, are produced in the summer.
Cultivation: Best grown in a soil bed well supplied with peat, as a humus-rich soil is enjoyed. Can be pot grown, though, in which case use a proprietary peat-based potting compost. When pot grown the stems can be twined around a system of canes or wire hoops. In summer give light shade and maintain a humid atmosphere. Water normally, but in autumn and winter allow the soil or compost to almost dry out before applying water. Feed fortnightly in summer with a liquid fertilizer. Good light is needed in winter. No pruning is necessary. If plants are cut back they are slow to recover, so if a plant becomes too large it is better to replace it with a young specimen.

JASMINUM Jasmine

Temperature: 4.5°C (40°F).
Characteristics: The jasmines create a heady atmosphere in the conservatory during the spring or summer with their deliciously fragrant flowers. The most easily obtainable species is the white-flowered *J. polyanthum*. Very attractive, though, are the yellow-flowered *J. primulinum* and *J. mesnyi*, so these are well worth looking out for.
Cultivation: The jasmines are easy to grow and do well in a soil bed or in pots. In the

summer they like an airy atmosphere and light shade from strong sunshine. Water as required throughout the year. You may need to prune in late winter if growth becomes congested or if you wish to contain the plant. Thin out older growth and leave as much younger wood as possible which will produce flowers. Reduce the height if necessary but do not be too severe with the secateurs.

LAPAGERIA   Chilean bellflower
Temperature: 4.5–7°C (40–45°F).
Characteristics: *Lapageria rosea*, from Chile, must be the most popular climber of all time. It is evergreen and attains a height of about 3 m (10 ft). In late summer and autumn it produces large, tubular, waxy blooms in a beautiful shade of crimson. There is a white variety available but this is less popular.

Lapageria rosea is the national flower of Chile and was introduced to Britain in the middle of the last century when it justifiably caused something of a sensation among collectors of exotic plants.
Cultivation: Best grown in a soil bed but also suitable for large pots. Acid or lime-free soil or compost is needed, and if pot grown use a proprietary acid peat-based compost. Mix plenty of peat or leafmould into the soil bed before planting. Cultivation is straight-forward: good ventilation and light shade in summer, normal watering all year round, and no pruning.

MANDEVILLA   Chilean jasmine
Temperature: 7°C (45°F).
Characteristics: From Argentina, *Mandevilla laxa* (also known as *M. suaveolens*) is a tall climber which, in summer, bears fragrant white funnel-shaped flowers. It is deciduous.
Cultivation: The Chilean jasmine is not happy when grown in a pot, so plant in a soil bed. Otherwise cultivation is simple enough: airy conditions and light shade in the summer, and fortnightly feeds with a liquid fertilizer. Water normally and decrease in the autumn and winter, but do not allow soil to dry out. I find that pruning is not needed.

PASSIFLORA   Passion flower
Temperature: 10°C (50°F).
Characteristics: These vigorous climbers are easy to grow and ideal for the cool conservatory. They flower in the summer and have the most intricate floral structure. The best known is the common blue Passion flower, *P. caerulea*, but others I can recommend include *P. × caeruleoracemosa* with purple blooms; the deep pink *P. × exoniensis*; and the pink or light violet *P. quadrangularis*.
Cultivation: Ideally grow in a soil bed, but plants can be grown in pots of soil-based compost. In summer the plants like a humid atmosphere and light shade, together with ample watering. In autumn and winter water very sparingly, only when the soil/compost is starting to dry out. I would not recommend feeding as the plants are naturally very vigorous. Pruning can be carried out in late winter: when the plants become congested, thin out the oldest stems and leave the younger ones. The side shoots on the stems remaining can be cut back to within 15 cm (6 in) of their base. If you have only a small conservatory you may find that the Passion flowers are a bit too large.

PLUMBAGO
Temperature: 7°C (45°F).
Characteristics: The South African *Plumbago capensis* is an ideal climber for the small cool conservatory, attaining about 3 m (10 ft) in height. A succession of blue flowers is produced in summer and autumn. Also attractive is the white variety 'Alba', but this is not so easily available as the blue one – try a houseplant grower.
Cultivation: Grow in a soil bed or pot, using well-drained soil-based compost. Lightly shade from strong sunshine in summer, feed once a fortnight and water regularly. Keep the soil/compost only slightly moist during the autumn and winter. In late winter carrying out pruning: cut back the side shoots to within a few centimetres of their base and shorten the main stems by about one-third.

A brick pillar provides support for *Mandevilla boliviensis*, while *Acalypha wilkesiana roseomarginata* provides a purple background for the groups of pot plants, which include lilac and purple streptocarpus, orange aeschynanthus, red and yellow iresine, red-flowered hibiscus and *Asparagus sprengeri*.

STEPHANOTIS   Madagascar jasmine

Temperature: 13°C (55°F).

Characteristics: The evergreen *Stephanotis floribunda*, from Madagascar, is a vigorous climber with deliciously fragrant white waxy blooms from spring to autumn.

Cultivation: Due to its vigour it is best grown in a soil bed, but a large pot or tub could be used, and either soil-based or peat-based compost.

When grown in pots, the stems are often trained to wire hoops. Normal watering is needed all year round, plus fortnightly feeds in summer, light shade and a moderately humid atmosphere. If you wish to control the size of the plant, prune in late winter by cutting back lateral shoots and reducing the height of the main stems.

Flowering pot plants
Short-term plants

Most of these plants are raised annually from seeds and provide colour at various times of the year. They are discarded after flowering.

ANNUALS, HARDY

Temperature: Best in a very cool conservatory, which is just frost free: do not subject plants to high temperatures.

Characteristics: Various hardy annuals make excellent pot plants for flowering in the spring, such as clarkia, cornflower (*Centaurea cyanus*), *Echium plantagineum*, godetia, and *Lavatera trimestris*. Also try these biennials: Canterbury bells (*Campanula medium*), and foxgloves or digitalis.

Cultivation: Sow the seeds in late summer, but late spring for Canterbury bells and foxgloves. Germinate the seeds in a cold frame and prick off seedlings into 9 cm (3½ in) pots. Use well-drained soil-based potting compost. Grow on the young plants in a cold frame with plenty of ventilation. Canterbury bells and foxgloves are best grown out of doors and put into a cold frame in early autumn.

Pot on young plants in early to mid-autumn, using 12.5 cm (5 in) pots. Final potting into 15 cm (6 in) pots should be completed by late autumn. The plants are moved into the conservatory in early winter.

Do make sure the conservatory is well ventilated, and water the plants very carefully. The compost should be kept only slightly moist: if too wet the plants may rot off. When the plants start growing more rapidly in spring increase watering and feed with a liquid fertilizer about once a fortnight.

BROWALLIA

Temperature: 10°C (50°F).

Characteristics: Browallias freely produce their tubular flowers in the summer and make neat, dwarf compact plants. Varieties offered by seedsmen include 'Blue Troll', bright blue flowers with white eyes; 'White Troll', pure white; 'Marine Bells', dark marine blue; and 'Jingle Bells', shades of blue, lavender and white.

Cultivation: Sow seeds in the spring and prick out the seedlings individually into 7.5 cm (3 in) pots; in due course pot on into final 12.5 cm (5 in) pots. Soil-based or peat-based composts are suitable. Browallias like good light but should be shaded from strong sunshine. Water as required.

CALCEOLARIA   Slipper wort

Temperature: 7°C (45°F).

Characteristics: These are popular plants, producing large pouched flowers in brilliant colours during spring or early summer. Seedsmen offer many mixed strains, with flowers in shades of red, yellow, orange, etc, often attractively spotted. A currently popular variety is 'Anytime Mixed', which can be sown throughout the year.

Cultivation: Sow the seeds in early summer and as they are very small do not cover them with compost. Germinate them in a cold frame. The seedlings are pricked off into seed trays and before they become overcrowded are potted into 7.5 cm (3 in) pots. Grow on in a cold frame with plenty of ventilation. The frame lights can be taken off when the weather is fine. In autumn pot into 12.5 cm, (5 in) pots and move the plants into the conservatory. It is essential to keep calceolarias cool at all times and they will not need more than 7°C in the winter. Ventilate well and keep the compost steadily moist in winter but avoid very wet compost. Pot on the plants into final 15 cm (6 in) pots in late winter. Calceolarias can be grown equally well in soil-based or peat-based compost.

CAMPANULA Bellflower

Temperature: 10°C (50°F).

Characteristics: The chimney bellflower, *Campanula pyramidalis*, is a stately biennial plant for the cool conservatory with flower spikes to a height of about 1.2 m (4 ft) in summer. The flowers are blue but there is also a white-flowered form available.

Cultivation: Sow the seeds in early or mid-spring and germinate them in a cool propagator, with a temperature of about 15.5°C (60°F). When the seedlings are large enough to handle, prick them off individually into 7.5 cm (3 in) pots. Place them in a cold frame. The young plants will be better out of doors for the summer and returned to the frame in autumn. Pot on as necessary until the plants are in 15–25 cm (6–10 in) pots, but do not carry out potting in winter. Plants are taken into the conservatory when the flower spikes are developing. Canes may be needed to support the stems. I find campanulas grow equally well in soil-based or peat-based compost.

CAPSICUM Ornamental pepper

Temperature: 10°C (50°F).

Characteristics: Capsicums are grown for their ornamental fruits which are produced in the autumn and winter. Generally the fruits are cone-shaped but may be round in some varieties. They come in shades of red, yellow and orange. The varieties offered by seedsmen are dwarf plants and hybrids of *C. annuum* and *C. frutescens*. Some popular varieties include 'Holiday Time', 'Fips',

'Holiday Cheer' and 'Inferno'.

Cultivation: Sow the seeds in mid-spring and germinate in a heated propagating case. Prick out the seedlings into 7.5 cm (3 in) pots. Before they become pot-bound move on into final 12.5 cm (5 in) pots. Soil-based or peat-based composts are suitable. Provide good ventilation and shade from the sun. When the plants are in flower I spray them overhead with plain water each day to ensure good pollination and consequently a good 'set' of berries.

CELOSIA Prince of Wales' feathers

Temperature: 10°C (50°F).

Characteristics: I am a great admirer of *Celosia plumosa* with its feathery flower heads in the summer in shades of red, yellow, apricot and pink. Many strains are offered by seedsmen, including 'Geisha Mixed', 'Fairy Fountains', 'Apricot Brandy' with apricot-orange plumes, and 'Red Glitters', with brilliant red plumes. They are dwarf pot plants, averaging 30 cm (12 in) in height.

Cultivation: Seeds are sown in early or mid-spring and should be germinated in a heated propagating case. Prick out the seedlings individually into 7.5 cm (3 in) pots and, before they become pot bound, pot on into final 12.5 cm (5 in) pots. Use soil-based or well-drained peat-based compost. Celosias like good light but will need shade from the strongest sun. Regular feeding in summer ensures really strong plants. Water normally but do not allow the compost to become saturated.

CHRYSANTHEMUM

Temperature: Cool or unheated conservatory.

Characteristics: Greenhouse chrysanthemums rank among the most important plants for autumn colour in the conservatory. The various types available and their cultivation constitute a very big subject and indeed there are many books devoted to chrysanthemums. Suffice to say here that there are large-flowered chrysanthemums like the greenhouse decoratives, single-flowered kinds like large daisies, and small-flowered spray and anemone-centred kinds. When making a choice of varieties it is best to consult a catalogue from a specialist chrysanthemum grower.

Cultivation: Plants are pot-grown, using soil-based compost. Early in the year rooted cuttings are potted into small pots, and are gradually potted on until they are in final 20 cm (8 in) pots. I always use soil-based compost. Young plants are grown on in a cold frame from early spring onwards, and from early summer onwards are grown out of doors.

The young plants should be stopped or pinched out when about 15 cm (6 in) high. Plenty of water and feeding is needed in summer, and in early autumn the plants are arranged in the conservatory to flower, when plenty of ventilation must be given to keep the air dry. The old flowered plants are cut down and kept over the winter in a cold frame to give cuttings in the following spring.

I think the charm chrysanthemums are superb conservatory plants. They make bushy specimens about 45 cm (18 in) in height and cover themselves with small flowers in many colours. They can be raised from cuttings or from seeds early in the year and are grown in the same way as the other greenhouse kinds.

EXACUM

Temperature: 13°C (55°F).
Characteristics: A popular, small, bushy annual, *Exacum affine* blooms in summer and autumn, covering itself with small starry bluish-purple blooms. 'Starlight Fragrance' is a good variety with scented flowers, and is available from seedsmen.
Cultivation: Sow seeds in early or mid-spring and germinate in a heated propagating case. Prick off seedlings into trays and then transfer to 10 cm (4 in) pots. Use soil-based or peat-based compost. Provide airy conditions, water as necessary and shade from sun.

IMPATIENS Busy lizzie
Temperature: 10°C(50°F).
Characteristics: Modern strains of impatiens are low-growing and compact. There are many to choose from, with flowers in brilliant colours, including red, pink, orange and white shades. Flowering is continuous throughout summer and well into autumn. The new Double Rosette impatiens are particularly attractive, with double flowers and highly recommended is the modern 'Super Elfin' strain in a wide range of colours.
Cultivation: Sow the seeds in early or mid-spring and germinate in heat. Prick off seedlings direct into 9 cm (3½ in) pots and later move into final 12.5 cm (5 in) pots. Use peat-based or soil-based compost. Impatiens like light shade, moisture and humidity.

IPOMOEA Morning glory
Temperature: 10°C(50°F).
Characteristics: *Ipomoea tricolor* is an annual climber with large saucer-shaped blooms in shades such as blue, lavender and white. The blue varieties are most popular, though, like 'Heavenly Blue' and 'Sapphire Cross'.
Cultivation: Sow seeds in early or mid-spring, one per 7.5 cm (3 in) pot, and germinate in a propagating case. Pot on young plants until they are in 20 cm (8 in) pots. Use well-drained soil-based compost. Good light is needed, but shade from strong sun. Provide supports.

PRIMULA

Temperature: 7–10°C (45–50°F). Certainly no higher than this.
Characteristics: Primulas are popular spring-flowering pot plants for the cool conservatory and are easily grown. The most popular are varieties of *P. obconica* with clusters of blooms in shades of red, pink, orange, blue, lilac and white. *P. malacoides*, popularly known as the fairy primrose, has tiers of star-shaped flowers in shades of red, mauve, pink, lilac and white. Yellow bell-shaped blooms are produced by the hybrid *P. × kewensis*, whose young leaves and flower

Part of Denis and Audrey Hayes' delightful conservatory (p.56), with pelargoniums, begonias, fuchsias and capsicums providing colour. A variegated ivy in the background adds further colour, while in front of this grow large succulents and Christmas cacti.

stems are covered with a white powdery meal.

Cultivation: Sowing time for these primulas varies: sow *P. obconica* in early or mid-spring; *P. malacoides* in late spring or early summer; and *P. × kewensis* in late winter or early spring. Germinate in cool conditions: 15.5°C (60°F). Prick out seedlings into trays, then transfer to 9 cm (3½ in) pots. Final pot size is 12.5 cm (5 in). From early summer to early autumn grow in a cold frame, keeping the plants well ventilated, shaded and moist. Take into the conservatory in early autumn and provide airy cool conditions and good light. Keep the compost steadily moist in winter but avoid wetting the foliage. A peat-based compost is ideal for primulas.

SALPIGLOSSIS Painted tongue

Temperature: 7°C (45°F).

Characteristics: *Salpiglossis sinuata* is a virtually hardy annual which blooms in summer and autumn, producing funnel-shaped blooms in a wide range of colours, generally multi-coloured.

Cultivation: Sow seeds in early spring and germinate in a heated propagating case. Prick out into 7.5 cm (3 in) pots and pot on to final 12.5 cm (5 in) pots. Use well-drained soil-based compost. Twiggy sticks may be needed to support the stems. Shade plants from strong sun and carry out normal watering.

SCHIZANTHUS Poor man's orchid

Temperature: 7–10°C (45–50°F). No higher as cool conditions needed.

Characteristics: This is an annual for the cool conservatory with orchid-like blooms in a wide range of colours. Many strains are available from seedsmen. Plants can be flowered at various times of year, but most people aim for winter or spring flowering.

Cultivation: For winter or spring flowering sow seeds in late summer and germinate in cool conditions such as a cold frame. Prick off into trays, and pot on into 9 cm (3½ in) pots. Split canes will be needed for support, or

twiggy sticks. Grow in a well-ventilated cold frame and transfer to the conservatory in autumn. Pot on in late winter into 15 cm (6 in) pots. Use well-drained soil-based compost. Maintain cool airy conditions and take care with watering – the compost must not be kept wet.

SENECIO Cineraria

Temperature: 7–10°C (45–50°F). No higher as cool conditions needed.

Characteristics: Popular plants for the cool conservatory, varieties of *Senecio × hybridus* have large heads of daisy-like flowers on neat compact plants. Colours include pink, red, blue, purple and white, and flowering time is late winter and spring.

Cultivation: Sow seeds from mid-spring to early summer and germinate in a cold frame. Prick off into trays and then pot on into 9 cm (3½ in) pots. Final pot size is 12.5 cm (5 in). Use well-drained compost, soil-based or peat-based. Grow in a cold frame in well-ventilated, cool, shaded, moist conditions. Move into the conservatory in early autumn, which should be cool and airy. Take care that the compost does not become too wet and avoid wetting the foliage.

SOLANUM Winter cherry

Temperature: 7°C (45°F).

Characteristics: The varieties of *Solanum capsicastrum* and *S. pseudocapsicum* produce red, orange or orange-red berries in the autumn and winter. Seedsmen offer many varieties such as 'Dwarf Red' and 'Red Giant'.

Cultivation: Sow seeds in late winter or early spring and germinate in a heated propagating case. Prick off into 7.5 cm (3 in) pots. Final pot size is 12.5 cm (5 in). Use well-drained soil-based compost. Pinch out growing tips of young plants to ensure bushy specimens. Grow out of doors for the summer and spray plants daily with water when in flower to ensure good pollination and therefore a good crop of berries. Transfer to the conservatory in early autumn and provide airy conditions.

Long-term plants

These pot plants can be kept for several or many years, according to type.

ANTHURIUM

Temperature: 15.5°C (60°F).

Characteristics: These plants come from the tropics – Central and South America – and are evergreen perennials producing colourful spathes. These are scarlet or orange-red in the popular *A. andreanum*; and bright scarlet in *A. scherzerianum*.

Cultivation: These plants like warm, humid, shady conditions, resembling the rain forests from which they originate. The compost should be kept steadily moist but only slightly moist in winter. I find a peat-based compost is the best growing medium. In winter, if the minimum temperature cannot be maintained, transfer plants to a warm room indoors.

BEGONIA

Temperature: 13–15.5°C (55–60°F).

Characteristics: Begonias can be had in flower at various times of the year. For winter there are the tuberous-rooted 'Gloire de Lorraine' hybrids in pink, yellow or orange shades; and the double-flowered 'Elatior' hybrids in shades of pink, red, peach and white. The fibrous-rooted *B. semperflorens*, the wax begonia, can flower all the year round, and there are many varieties in shades of red, pink and white. There are many begonias with cane-like stems such as *B. corallina* with silver-spotted leaves and pink flowers from spring to autumn.

There are one or two nurserymen who specialise in begonias so if you want some of the more unusual ones you will have to buy mail-order.

Cultivation: Begonias grow particularly well in peat-based composts. Be careful with watering, allowing the compost to partially dry out between applications. Provide a humid atmosphere, particularly when temperatures are high; ensure good light but shade from strong sunshine.

CARNIVOROUS PLANTS

Temperature: 4.5°C (40°F).

Characteristics: The temperate species of carnivorous plants (plants which trap insects) are becoming very popular and are ideal plants for the cool conservatory. The easiest to grow include the cobra lily, *Darlingtonia californica*, with tall yellowish-green pitchers (in which insects are trapped); the trumpet pitchers, such as *Sarracenia flava* with tall pale green pitchers; and the Venus fly trap, *Dionaea muscipula*, with jaw-like traps which close when insects land on them.

Cultivation: Keep plants cool in winter and the compost only slightly moist. In spring and summer keep the compost wet, but not waterlogged, and ensure high humidity. Use rainwater or soft tap water for watering. Provide good ventilation and light, but shade from strong sunshine. Pot in spring if necessary, using plastic pots and a compost of peat and Perlite in equal parts.

CLIVIA

Temperature: 7°C (45°F).

Characteristics: *Clivia miniata* is an evergreen perennial from Natal with long strap-shaped leaves and heads of orange funnel-shaped blooms in spring or summer. In the wild it grows in harsh scrubland conditions.

Cultivation: An easily grown plant for the cool conservatory. Best growth is obtained by growing it in a soil bed, but it can also be pot grown. It does not like root disturbance as the roots are fleshy, so take care with potting on. Use a well-drained soil-based compost. Water normally in summer, but in winter allow the compost to almost dry out before watering. High humidity is appreciated in warm conditions and shade from strong sunshine.

CYMBIDIUM Orchids

Temperature: 10°C (50°F).

Characteristics: The cymbidium orchids are easily grown in the cool conservatory. There are many hybrids available, including miniatures, and they flower in winter and spring. Many colours are available.

Cultivation: These plants need really good ventilation in summer. Shade from hot sun, spray the plants with water in warm conditions and liquid feed in the summer. Keep the compost steadily moist. When the plants have really filled their pots, pot on in the spring, using a compost of equal parts bark and peat, with some pieces of charcoal added to keep it 'sweet'.

ERICA   Heather

Temperature: 7°C (45°F).

Characteristics: The most popular of the greenhouse heathers is *E. × hyemalis*, a dwarf evergreen shrub with pink and white flowers in the autumn and winter.

Cultivation: An ideal pot plant for the cool conservatory with airy conditions. Plants are best kept out of doors for the summer, returning them to the conservatory in early autumn. Keep the compost steadily moist at all times, and apply liquid feeds in summer. Heathers must have an acid or lime-free, peat-based compost. Allow them to become slightly pot-bound before potting on.

EUPHORBIA   Poinsettia

Temperature: 15.5°C (60°F).

Characteristics: The winter-flowering poinsettia is correctly *Euphorbia pulcherrima*, which produces spectacular leaf-like bracts in scarlet, pink or cream. It is found in the wild in Central America, particularly Mexico.

Cultivation: This is not one of the easiest conservatory plants, unless you can maintain a steady temperature of 15.5°C (60°F). Most people buy plants round about Christmas time and discard them after flowering, because they are difficult to get into flower again, but they are truly perennial. Poinsettias like good light, shade from strong sun and moderate humidity. Water well in summer but allow compost to partially dry out between applications in winter. After flowering, cut down the stems to 15 cm (6 in) and keep the plants virtually dry until late spring to rest them.

FUCHSIA

Temperature: 4.5°C (40°F).

Characteristics: There are many hundreds of varieties of fuchsia in a wide range of colours. They are shrubby plants and there are various ways of growing them. Many can be grown as bush plants; strong-growing varieties as standards or fan shapes; and pendulous kinds in hanging baskets.

Fuchsias provide a continuous display throughout the summer.

Cultivation: Most people raise new plants each year and discard the old plants. Soft cuttings root easily in spring or early summer, to provide flowering plants the following year.

Plants can be kept for several years, though, and eventually make large specimens. In this case they are rested over winter by keeping the compost only barely moist. In the following spring they are started into growth again by re-potting and increasing watering and temperature. Prune back all shoots to within two or three buds.

An impressive feature for the back wall of a conservatory is a fuchsia trained to a fan shape, and maybe up into the roof area, too. This should be planted in a soil bed and can remain there for many years. Choose a strong vigorous grower such as 'Mme Cornelissen'.

Fuchsias grow well in peat-based composts and young plants should be potted on until they are in 15–20 cm (6–8 in) pots. Airy conditions are needed, plus shade from strong sun, plenty of water when in growth, but far less in winter. Feed fortnightly in summer with a liquid fertilizer.

HYDRANGEA

Temperature: 7°C (45°F).

Characteristics: Varieties of the garden hydrangea, *H. macrophylla*, are excellent for the cool conservatory, producing their large mop-headed blooms in the spring. The flowers may be pink or blue. If you want blue flowers the plants should be grown in acid or lime-free compost.

A pool is not difficult to build in a conservatory and allows one to grow some exciting tender aquatics if heat is provided. The tall grassy-looking plant at the edge of this pool is *Cyperus alternifolius*. The ferny *Asparagus sprengeri* cascades into the water, and in the pool itself are tropical waterlilies and the water hyacinth.

Cultivation: Most people raise new plants each year by taking soft cuttings in the spring. Pot rooted cuttings into 9 cm (3½ in) pots, and later pot on into 12.5 cm (5 in) pots. Pinch out the tips of the young plants. Keep plants in a well-ventilated cold frame for the summer, shading them and keeping the compost moist. In the autumn return them to the conservatory and pot on to 15 cm (6 in) pots. Keep compost only just moist in winter. Maintain airy conditions.

PELARGONIUM

Temperature: 7–10°C (45–50°F).
Characteristics: The regal pelargonium, varieties of *P. domesticum*, are popular pot plants for summer display. There are many varieties available in shades of red, pink, purple, mauve and white.
Cultivation: New plants are generally raised each year from cuttings taken in late summer, the old plants being discarded at the end of the season. Pot off rooted cuttings into 9 cm (3½ in) pots. In early spring pot on to 12.5 cm (5 in) pots. I prefer to use a well-drained, soil-based compost for regal pelargoniums. Basic conditions consist of plenty of light and sun, but keep shaded from very strong sunshine. Maintain a dry and airy atmosphere all year round. Water and liquid feed well in the growing season, but in winter keep the compost only slightly moist.

SAINTPAULIA   African violet

Temperature: Maintain a steady temperature in the range 18–24°C (65–75°F).
Characteristics: There are a great many varieties of *S. ionantha*, with single and double blooms in many colours, including shades of blue, purple, violet, pink, red and white. All are very neat, low-growing plants with rosettes of leaves.
Cultivation: Grow plants in half pots or pans as they are shallow rooting, and in peat-based compost. Allow to become slightly pot-bound before potting on. The plants will need to be shaded from strong sun, although they do like some sunshine. High

humidity is essential. Keep the compost moist at all times. Best to water from below as the foliage must be kept dry.

STRELITZIA   Bird of paradise flower

Temperature: 7°C (45°F).
Characteristics: *Strelitzia reginae*, a native of South Africa, has flamboyant orange and blue flowers in summer, which are shaped rather like a bird's head, and large banana-like leaves. It grows to a height of about 1.5 m (5 ft)
Cultivation: Eventually the plant will need a large pot or tub, but the alternative is to grow it in a soil bed. When pot grown use a soil-based compost. This plant needs plenty of sun and very airy conditions. Feed well in the summer water normally, but keep the soil/compost only slightly moist in winter. Young plants may take five years or more to flower, so be patient.

STREPTOCARPUS   Cape primrose

Temperature: 7–10°C (45–50°F).
Characteristics: These are popular evergreen perennials which flower in summer, bearing funnel-shaped or tubular blooms, purple-blue in variety 'Constant Nymph', and in various colours in the John Innes hybrids. The 'Concorde' strain is also recommended, producing small compact plants in a mixture of colours.
Cultivation: In summer, shade from strong sun and provide high humidity. Water normally in spring and summer but in winter keep the compost dryish.

Foliage pot plants

AGLAEONEMA

Temperature: 13°C (55°F).
Characteristics: From the tropical forests of south-east Asia, aglaeonema species are evergreen perennials with large leaves and most are low-growing plants. The one most usually offered is *A. commutatum* whose green leaves are speckled with silver grey. It has some attractive varieties, like 'Pseudobracteatum' (also known as 'White Rajah'), and 'Silver

Queen', both boldly marked with white.
Cultivation: Provide warm humid conditions and avoid direct sun as these are shade-loving plants. Water well in spring and summer but keep the compost dryish in autumn and winter. Feed fortnightly in the growing period. Growth is good in peat-based composts.

ASPARAGUS   Asparagus ferns
Temperature: 10°C (50°F).
Characteristics: These African evergreen perennials are not true ferns, although they have ferny foliage, making a nice foil for brightly coloured flowering pot plants. Popular species are *A. plumosus*; *A. sprengeri*; and *A. asparagoides*. *A. sprengeri* is excellent for hanging baskets, or it can be allowed to trail over the edge of the staging. The other species can be trained to upright supports, such as pot trellis.
Cultivation: Provide a humid atmosphere in warm conditions, water normally all year round, and shade from hot sun. Regular feeding in summer is beneficial. A soil-based or peat-based compost is suitable. Pot on plants in the spring but bear in mind large pots are not needed.

BEGONIA
Temperature: 15.5°C (60°F).
Characteristics: There are many begonias, of tropical origin, with attractive foliage and all are evergreen perennials. Very popular, with marbled, maple-like leaves are *B.* × 'Cleopatra' and *B.* × 'Tiger'. Others have red-flushed leaves, particularly on the undersides, like *B. erythrophylla* and *B. luxurians*. The most popular of all, though, are the iron-cross begonia, *B. masoniana*, with a deep purple cross in the centre of the leaves, and the multicoloured *B. rex*.
Cultivation: Provide high humidity in warm conditions, shade from direct sunshine, and feed once a fortnight in summer. Take care with watering – apply water only when the compost is drying out, and reduce further in winter. Grow in peat-based potting compost.

BROMELIADS   Air plants, urn plants and earth stars
Temperature: 10°C (50°F).
Characteristics: The bromeliads, members of the pineapple family, are rapidly gaining in popularity and are destined to become as popular as cacti and succulents. Most of those we grow come from the tropical rain forests of South America, yet are very adaptable under cultivation.

The air plants or atmospheric tillandsias are epiphytic plants, growing on trees in the wild, and they absorb moisture through their leaves. They are small plants and very variable in habit: *T. caput-medusae*, *T. butzii* and *T. baileyi* are bulbous and have contorted leaves; *T. juncea* has rush like leaves; *T. ionantha* forms contorted rosettes; *T. argentea* has fine silvery leaves; and *T. usneoides*, the Spanish moss, consists of green threads.

The ground-dwelling earth stars or cryptanthus are attractive bromeliads, with flat rosettes of striped, barred or mottled leaves. The popular epiphytic *Vriesia splendens*, or flaming sword, has a rosette of brown-banded leaves forming a 'vase' shape. The flower head consists of scarlet bracts and yellow flowers. Also forming 'vases' are *Guzmannia lingulata* with orange or red flower spikes, and *Nidularium fulgens*, with a bright red centre and a flower spike consisting of red bracts and violet flowers. Both the latter-named plants are epiphytic.

The ornamental pineapple, *Ananas comosus* 'Variegatus', forms a wide rosette of narrow spiny leaves edged with cream. It is a ground dweller.

Other popular epiphytic bromeliads are *Tillandsia cyanea*, the pink quill, with a rosette of green leaves and a flower head of pink bracts and blue flowers; *Billbergia nutans*, queen's tears, which forms a clump of dark green grassy leaves and has green, pink and blue flowers among pink bracts; and *Aechmea fasciata*, the urn plant, which forms a tall rosette of wide, grey-green banded leaves forming a 'vase', and has blue or lilac flowers among pink bracts.

Cultivation: The atmospheric tillandsias cannot be grown in pots – instead grow them on pieces of wood or on a 'plant tree'. Either gently wedge them into nooks and crannies, or tie into place with clear nylon thread. Lightly mist spray the plants daily in warm conditions, or once a week in cool conditions. Use rainwater or soft water. Provide good indirect light and plenty of fresh air.

The other bromeliads mentioned can be pot grown, using a well-drained peat-based compost. Use small pots and pot on only when plants are pot bound. The epiphytic bromeliads could, alternatively, be grown on a 'plant tree'.

Keep the compost moist all year round but not wet. Provide very high humidity in warm conditions, but less in cool conditions. Provide good light but shade from sunshine. Those bromeliads which form water-holding 'vases' should have their vases filled with water. Replace it frequently to keep it fresh. Always use rainwater or soft water for bromeliads, as hard alkaline water can kill them.

The pineapple needs very good light, even direct sunshine, for the best leaf colour. It should be watered moderately, and in winter very sparingly – only enough to prevent the compost from drying out completely. Use clay pots and pot on every two years, using soil-based compost with extra peat.

CALATHEA

Temperature: 10°C (50°F).
Characteristics: The calatheas are evergreen perennials from the tropical rain forests of South America. All have beautifully marked leaves and any of the following species are well worth acquiring: *C. lancifolia*, *C. makoyana*, *C. ornata* and *C. zebrina*.
Cultivation: Calatheas like plenty of warmth and will only 'tick over' in the minimum temperature. High humidity is necessary plus shade from the sun. Water normally in summer and feed once a fortnight, but give less water in winter. Growth is good in peat-based composts.

CHLOROPHYTUM   Spider plant
Temperature: 7°C (45°F).
Characteristics: *Chlorophytum comosum* 'Variegatum' is a popular evergreen perennial with green and white striped grassy leaves. Small plants develop on the ends of the old flower stems and form a cascade of growth. At this stage the plant is ideal for hanging containers or for the edge of the staging.
Cultivation: As it is a fast grower annual potting on may be necessary, using well-drained, soil-based compost. Water and feed well in summer; apply less water in autumn and winter. Shade from strong sun but ensure good light for best colour. Best conditions are warmth and humidity.

CISSUS   Kangaroo vine
Temperature: 4.5°C (40°F).
Characteristics: *Cissus antarctica*, from Australia, is an evergreen climber with deep green glossy leaves. It is of modest stature and suitable for most conservatories.
Cultivation: Best grown in soil-based potting compost. The stems will need adequate supports. In summer provide high humidity and shade from strong sunshine – a good plant for a shady situation. Be careful with watering; allow the compost to dry out partially between applications. Feed fortnightly in the growing season. Pinch out the growing tips to encourage bushy plants. Prune back in late winter if the plant becomes too tall.

CODIAEUM   Croton
Temperature: 15.5°C (60°F).
Characteristics: *Codiaeum variegatum pictum*, a native of the warm humid forests of Malaysia and the Pacific islands, has produced many varieties. The leaves are of various shapes, sizes and colours, many being highly coloured in shades of red, orange, pink, yellow and copper. The leaves of many varieties are multicoloured. There are probably no better plants for creating a lush tropical effect in the conservatory.

By far the most attractive and easiest way of growing epiphytic bromeliads is on a section of tree. The pot-grown bromeliads have been plunged in a layer of pine needles.

Cultivation: Plenty of warmth and high humidity are the main requirements. Ensure good light for the best colour, but provide shade from strong sunshine. Water normally in summer but less in winter, and liquid feed fortnightly during the growing season. Soil-based potting compost is recommended.

COLEUS   Flame nettle
Temperature: 10°C (50°F).
Characteristics: Varieties of *Coleus blumei* have nettle-like leaves in many colours — some have leaves of one colour, others are multicoloured. Most seedsmen offer a good range of varieties.
Cultivation: Most people treat coleus as short-term plants, discarding them at the end of the season and raising new plants from seeds in the spring. They can also be raised from cuttings. Good light is needed for the best leaf colour, but shade from strong sun. High humidity should be provided in high temperatures. Water well in summer and feed fortnightly. Pinch out the growing tips of young plants to ensure bushy specimens. Also remove the flowers. Best grown in soil-based potting compost.

CORDYLINE
Temperature: 15.5°C (60°F).
Characteristics: From the tropical rain forests of India, *Cordyline terminalis* has large lanceolate leaves, bronzy red or purplish, but cream edged with pink when young. A most attractive variety is 'Tricolor' with cream, pink and red leaves.
Cultivation: Warm humid conditions are needed and, in summer, light shade. Water and feed well in the growing period, but reduce watering in winter. Use a soil-based potting compost.

CTENANTHE
Temperature: 10°C (50°F).
Characteristics: Ctenanthes originate from the rain forests of South America and the best known is *C. oppenheimiana* 'Tricolor', an evergreen perennial with long leaves marked with white, and bright red on the undersides.
Cultivation: Plenty of warmth and high humidity are needed for best growth, and shade from sun. Feed and water normally in the growing period, but water sparingly in winter. A soil-based compost is best, with extra peat added.

DIEFFENBACHIA   Dumb cane
Temperature: 15.5°C (60°F).
Characteristics: These tropical evergreen perennials from Central and South America have large leaves which are heavily patterned with white or cream. Popular kinds are *D. maculata* and *D. exotica*.
Cultivation: Plenty of warmth and humidity, good light for best leaf colour but shade from sunshine. Normal watering throughout the year, fortnightly feeding in growing season. Best grown in soil-based compost with extra peat.

DRACAENA
Temperature: 13°C (55°F).
Characteristics: The dracaenas are evergreen shrubs from tropical Africa and are very variable in habit. Most popular are *D. deremensis* and its varieties with green and silver (or white) striped, sword-shaped leaves. Palm-like is *D. marginata* from Madagascar, with long thin leaves. Variety 'Tricolor' is striped cream and pink.
Cultivation: Warmth, high humidity and in summer light shade are the main requirement. Feed and water well in the growing period; water more sparingly in winter. I prefer to use soil-based potting compost.

FERNS
Temperature: 10°C (50°F).
Characteristics: The various kinds of ferns, generally with plain green but attractively cut leaves or fronds, are traditional conservatory plants and are used mainly as a foil for brightly coloured pot plants. Ferns were very popular with the Victorians and are an excellent choice for Victorian-style conservatories. Ferns suitable for the minimum

In a temperate conservatory, summer colour provided by trained pot-grown bougainvilleas (*foreground*), large pot-grown coleus for coloured foliage, streptocarpus, and golden-leaved helxine. At the back of the group *Grevillea robusta* provides fresh ferny foliage.

temperature of 10°C (50°F) include the adiantums or maidenhair ferns; *Asplenium bulbiferum*, the spleenwort; *Cyrtomium falcatum*, the holly fern; *Diksonia antarctica*, the tree fern; *Nephrolepis exaltata*, the sword fern, excellent for hanging baskets; *Platycerium bifurcatum*, the staghorn fern, ideal for hanging containers; and *Pteris cretica* and *P. tremula*, the table ferns.

Cultivation: Shade ferns from direct sun as it can cause the fronds to shrivel. High humidity is needed in warm conditions, plus an airy atmosphere. Keep the compost steadily moist all year round and feed fortnightly in summer. A peat-based potting compost is suitable for ferns.

FICUS   Rubber plants and figs

Temperature: 15.5°C (60°F).

Characteristics: This is a diverse genus which contains trees, shrubs, climbers and trailing plants. The following are excellent plants for the conservatory: *F. benjamina*, the weeping fig from South East Asia, is a small pendulous tree with shiny oval leaves; *F. elastica* 'Decora' is the well-known rubber plant with large leathery deep green glossy leaves; *F. lyrata* is the fiddle-back fig from tropical West Africa, a tree with huge spoon-shaped leaves, deep glossy green; and *F. pumila*, the creeping fig from China and Japan, with small green heart-shaped leaves, which can be grown as a climber or trailer.

Cultivation: Requirements are straight-forward: warm humid conditions, light shade from strong sun, regular feeding in summer, normal watering, but allow compost to dry out partially in winter. Use a soil-based or peat-based compost.

GREVILLEA   Silk oak

Temperature: 4.5°C (40°F).

Characteristics: *Grevillea robusta* grows into a tall tree in its native Queensland and New South Wales, but under glass it makes a manageable specimen in a pot. It has ferny green leaves with silky undersides.

Cultivation: The silk oak likes an airy atmosphere and plenty of light, but shade from the hottest sun. Carry out normal watering but reduce in winter. Use an acid or lime-free soil-based compost and carry out annual potting-on as growth is rapid.

HEDERA   Ivy

Temperature: 4.5°C (40°F); also suitable for unheated conservatory.

Characteristics: There are many varieties of our native *Hedera helix*, with plain green or variegated leaves. They can be grown as climbers but are very attractive when grown in hanging containers, or allowed to cascade over the edge of the staging. Larger-leaved ivies include *H. canariensis* 'Gloire de Marengo', the variegated Canary Island ivy.

Cultivation: These ivies are hardy plants so can be grown without heat. At any rate they prefer cool conditions, an airy atmosphere and humidity in warm weather. Shade plants from the sun but give variegated ivies good light for best leaf colour. The green-leaved kinds are ideal for shady places. Carry out normal watering in summer but be very sparing with water in winter or roots may rot. Feed fortnightly in growing season. Use soil-based or peat-based potting compost.

MARANTA   Prayer plant

Temperature: 10°C (50°F).

Characteristics: *Maranta leuconeura* is a low-growing spreading evergreen perennial from Brazil, whose leaves have bluish green veins and purple undersides. There are several varieties with intricately patterned leaves, like 'Erythroneura', red veins, purple undersides; 'Kerchoveana', leaves spotted reddish brown; and 'Massangeana', with silvery veins.

Cultivation: Marantas need warm humid conditions in order to flourish. Shade from direct sun but ensure good light in the winter. Carry out normal watering in the growing season, but sparingly in winter. Feed fortnightly in summer. Best results in peat-based compost. Use half pots or pans, or grow in hanging baskets.

MONSTERA   Swiss cheese plant

Temperature: 15.5°C (60°F).

Characteristics: The popular *Monstera deliciosa* is a rain-forest climber from Mexico and various other parts of tropical America. To create a lush tropical effect in the conservatory there are few plants to equal it. The huge leaves are deeply cut and perforated, although young ones do not have this characteristic. Aerial roots are produced from the thick stems.

Cultivation: Monstera is best grown up a thick moss pole, into which the aerial roots will grow. Warm humid conditions are best together with shade from strong sun. Water moderately throughout the year and pot on regularly as growth is vigorous. Use a soil-based compost with extra peat. Feed fortnightly in the growing season.

PALMS

Temperature: 10–13°C (50–55°F).

Characteristics: No conservatory is complete without a palm and I would suggest choosing some of the larger kinds rather than dwarf palms. *Howea belmoreana* and *H. forsterana*, which grow in temperate forests of Lord Howe Island (in the South Pacific), have well-divided feathery foliage held on tall stems. Not so tall is *Phoenix canariensis*, the Canary Island date palm, with stiff, prickly fronds.

Cultivation: Palms grow in good light to slight shade, but protect them from strong sunshine. Water well in the growing season but sparingly in winter when the plants are resting. A fortnightly feed in summer encourages good growth. Use a soil-based compost and pot on every two years until a large pot or tub is reached.

PEPEROMIA   Pepper elder

Temperature: 13–15.5°C (55–60°F).

Characteristics: These dwarf evergreen perennials, with varied but attractive leaves, come from the rain forest of Central and South America and the West Indies. Some have deep green crinkled leaves, like *P.*

caperata; others are banded silver and green such as *P. argyreia*; and there are some with thick fleshy leaves, such as *P. obtusifolia*, these being variegated in the varieties 'Green Gold' and 'Variegata'.

Cultivation: Try to provide rain-forest conditions (but without the rain): in other words, plenty of warmth and high humidity. Shade from sun but ensure good light. The compost should be allowed to almost dry out between waterings and spring and summer feeding is recommended. Plants grow well, I find, in all-peat composts, and they are best grown in half pots or pans as they have shallow root systems. Do not over-pot.

PHILODENDRON

Temperature: 15.5°C (60°F).

Characteristics: Like monsteras, palms and ficus, the philodendrons are, in my opinion, essential conservatory plants, creating a lush 'jungle' atmosphere. There are shrubby and climbing species and they come from the South American rain forests. They have large and handsome leaves and many species produce long aerial roots from the stems. Some of my favourites include *P. bipinnatifidum*, with deeply cut leaves; the climbing *P. elegans*, also with deeply cut foliage; the climbing *P. erubescens*, with copper-flushed leaves; *P. hastatum*, a climber with shiny green foliage; the climbing *P. laciniatum*, with lobed leaves; and *P. scandens*, a climber with heart-shaped leaves. There are also some attractive named varieties like the climbing 'Burgundy' with red-flushed foliage, and 'Tuxla', also a climber, with shiny green foliage.

Cultivation: The climbing kinds will need supports such as a thick moss pole into which they can bury their aerial roots. Trellis, or something similar, could also be used, the roots then being trained down into the soil. *P. scandens* is a good plant for a hanging basket. Warmth, high humidity and shade from the sun are the main requirements. Water normally in the growing season but apply far less in winter. Fortnightly feeds in spring and summer are beneficial. I use a compost of equal parts soil-based compost and peat.

SANSEVIERIA   Mother-in-law's tongue

Temperature: 10°C (50°F).
Characteristics: The South African *Sansevieria trifasciata* is a remarkably tough plant, and has stiff, upright, sword-like leaves, rather fleshy. These are deep green with cross bands of lighter green. The more popular *S. t.* 'Laurentii' has yellow-edged leaves.
Cultivation: Provide very good light but shade from the hottest sun, and a dry atmosphere. Water with care – only apply water when the compost is drying out. Allow to become slightly pot-bound before potting on, and use a well-drained soil-based compost.

SCINDAPSUS

Temperature: 15.5°C (60°F).
Characteristics: These evergreen climbers are similar to some philodendrons and also produce aerial roots. Popular is *S. aureus* from Australasia, with oval leaves marbled yellow. The form called 'Marble Queen' has cream, green and grey-green foliage. *S. pictus* 'Argyraeus' from Malaya and Borneo has silver-grey spotted foliage.
Cultivation: This is the same as for philodendrons. Plants can be allowed to climb or to trail from hanging baskets.

TRADESCANTIA   Wandering Jew

Temperature: 7°C (45°F).
Characteristics: Very common trailing evergreen perennial (but not to be despised for that), suitable for hanging containers and for cascading over the edge of the staging. There are several plain green and variegated varieties available, but one of my favourites is *T. fluminensis* 'Quicksilver' whose leaves have bold white and green stripes.
Cultivation: Provide good light but shade from hot sun. Water normally in the growing period but keep much drier in winter, especially in low temperatures. Feed well in summer. Grow in soil-based or peat-based compost. Best to replace plants regularly with young specimens – cuttings root very easily in spring or summer.

ZEBRINA   Wandering Jew

Temperature: 7°C (45°F).
Characteristics: Similar habit and uses to tradescantia. *Z. pendula* from Central America has silver-banded leaves, purple below. Better are the varieties 'Purpusii', green flushed with purple, and 'Quadricolor', leaves banded with pink, red and white.
Cultivation: This is the same as for tradescantia.

Bulbous and tuberous plants

BEGONIA

Temperature: 13°C (55°F).
Characteristics: The tuberous begonias make a highly colourful display in the conservatory during the summer. They have large double flowers in a wide range of strong and pastel colours. There are also pendulous varieties which are excellent subjects for hanging baskets.
Cultivation: The tubers are started into growth in late winter or early spring. They are pressed into moist peat in a seed tray and ideally placed in a warm propagating case. Shoots will soon start to appear, at which stage the tubers are potted into 12.5 cm (5 in) pots of soil-based or all-peat compost. The top of each tuber must be level with the compost.

Feed once a fortnight as soon as flower buds start to appear, and carry out normal watering. Shade from the sun.

The tubers can be kept for several years by drying off the plants in autumn, removing the tubers and cleaning them, and storing in dry peat in a frost-proof place.

The tubers must be checked about once a month while in store and if any are rotting they should be removed.

An attractive grouping of tropical plants in a warm conservatory. In the foreground is *Ctenanthe oppenheimiana* 'Tricolor'. The blue flowers belong to *Dichorisandra veginae*. The plants in the background include coloured-leaved codiaeums and cordylines. An example of beautifully contrasting foliage.

CANNA   Indian shot lily

Temperature: 15.5°C (60°F).

Characteristics: Cannas grow from fleshy rhizomes, flower during summer and die down for the winter. The tubular flowers are quite spectacular, in shades of red, orange or yellow. Varieties of *C. × generalis* are generally grown, and their height is 60–90 cm (24–36 in).

Cultivation: The rhizomes are started into growth in the same way as begonias. When shoots appear, pot into suitable-sized pots, using a soil-based compost. Before the plants become pot-bound pot on into 15–22 cm (6–9 in) pots. Feed and water well in the summer. In autumn, gradually dry off the plants, cut down the top growth and store in their pots for the winter in frost-free conditions. The compost should not become bone dry in the winter.

CYCLAMEN

Temperature: 10°C (50°F).

Characteristics: The cyclamen, hybrids of *C. persicum*, are very popular autumn and winter-flowering pot plants which grow from tubers. There are many colours available including red, pink, purple, lilac and white. Some varieties have beautifully marbled foliage, and in recent years some delightful miniature varieties have appeared on the market. Some cyclamen have scented blooms, and others are frilly.

Cultivation: Cyclamen can be raised from seeds sown in late summer. They are pricked out into small pots, and potted on until eventually they are in 15 cm (6 in) pots. Peat-based potting compost gives good results. In the summer of the following year grow the young plants in a well-ventilated and shaded cold frame, and take into the conservatory in early autumn to flower. Bear in mind that cool airy conditions are needed at all times.

The tubers can be kept for many years. When the leaves start to die down dry off the plants and rest them in a cold frame. In late summer remove the tubers and re-pot into fresh compost. The top of the tuber must be above compost level. When watering cyclamen do not wet the centre of the plant or flower buds and leaf stalks may rot.

FREESIA

Temperature: 7°C (45°F).

Characteristics: Freesias are grown mainly for winter flowering and many have highly fragrant blooms. There are many colours available and flowers may be single or double. They are ideal plants for the cool conservatory, as high temperatures should be avoided at all times.

Cultivation: Plant corms in late summer, about eight to a 15 cm (6 in) pot, using a soil-based compost and inserting them 2.5 cm (1 in) deep. Place in a cold frame and cover the pots with peat. Within six weeks growth should have started, at which stage the pots are moved into the conservatory. Provide good light and ventilation and water moderately. The plants will need supporting with thin twiggy sticks. After flowering start to reduce watering and eventually allow the compost to become dry, to give plants a rest. In late summer, re-pot them into fresh compost and start into growth again.

GLORIOSA   Climbing lily

Temperature: 13°C (55°F).

Characteristics: *Gloriosa rothschildiana* from tropical Africa is a climber which grows from a tuber. It produces lily-like flowers in summer and these are crimson with yellow edges.

The climbing lily is now readily available from garden centres, the tubers, generally coming from Holland, being pre-packed.

Cultivation: Pot the tuber in spring, using a soil-based compost. Keep the compost only slightly moist at all times. Airy conditions are required, and light shade from strong sunshine. Feed fortnightly in the summer. Supports will be needed for the stems. The tubers are dried off in the autumn and stored for the winter in a temperature of 7–10°C (45–50°F).

HIPPEASTRUM

Temperature: 10°C (50°F).

Characteristics: Hippeastrums produce huge trumpet-shaped blooms, from equally large bulbs. Spring is the usual flowering time, although blooms may appear in winter if conditions are fairly warm. Colours may be crimson, scarlet, pink or white, and some varieties are bi-coloured.

Cultivation: The bulbs can be started off in early winter if you have a warm conservatory, otherwise start them in late winter. Plant a single bulb in a 15 cm (6 in) pot, leaving the top half exposed. Use a soil-based potting compost. Repot bulbs every three years. When flowering has finished, start feeding with a liquid fertilizer. In late summer the leaves will start to die down. At this stage reduce watering to give the bulbs a rest, keeping the compost only just moist.

HYACINTHS

Temperature: Suitable for cool or unheated conservatory.

Characteristics: Hyacinths are hardy bulbs which will flower in winter or early spring under glass. Specially prepared bulbs will produce their blooms in time for Christmas. Most varieties are deliciously scented.

Cultivation: Bulbs should be planted in early autumn, including those specially prepared for very early flowering. Generally they are planted in bulb bowls, using bulb fibre, with the tips of the bulbs just showing.

After planting, the bulbs are placed in a cool shady position out of doors and covered with a 15 cm (6 in) layer of peat. They need to be kept in a temperature below 9°C (48°F). After about eight weeks, when roots and shoots have developed, transfer the bulbs to the conservatory and provide a temperature of 10°C (50°F). In the case of prepared hyacinths, the temperature can be increased to 15.5°C (60°F) when the flower buds have formed, to speed up flowering. Do not force bulbs again, but plant them in the garden. I like to set groups of them in a shrub border, in full sun.

LILIUM Lily

Temperature: 10°C (50°F) – cool conditions are needed.

Characteristics: Various lilies make superb pot plants for the cool conservatory and as they are hardy can even be grown without heat. Those which I particularly recommend are *L. auratum* with white and yellow blooms; 'Enchantment', orange-red; the white Easter lily, *L. longiflorum*; *L. regale*, white and pink; and *L. speciosum rubrum*, pink and carmine.

Cultivation: Pot bulbs in autumn, using soil-based compost and well-crocked pots. Plant three bulbs per 20 cm (8 in) pot. All of the above lilies, except 'Enchantment', are stem-rooting and should be planted shallowly in half-filled pots. Later they are topdressed with more compost.

Keep the pots in a cold frame for the winter and transfer to the conservatory in early or mid-spring. Provide airy conditions. After flowering, place back in the frame and plant out in the garden in autumn.

NARCISSUS Daffodils

Temperature: Suitable for cool or unheated conservatory.

Characteristics: As with hyacinths, daffodils flower in the winter or early spring, and specially prepared bulbs bloom in time for Christmas. Daffodils are hardy so can be grown without heat if desired. There are many varieties to choose from, but still as popular as ever are the large, golden trumpet varieties.

Cultivation: As for hyacinths, the bulbs being planted in early autumn.

NERINE

Temperature: 7°C (45°F).

Characteristics: Nerines flower in the autumn and should be grown in cool conditions. The best-known species is *N. bowdenii* with pink blooms. Similar is *N. flexuosa*, while *N. sarniensis* has red or pink blooms and *N. undulata* is pink. There are many named varieties available, too.

Cultivation: Bulbs should be potted in late summer using a moist soil-based compost. Plant one per 9 cm (3½ in) pot, leaving the neck exposed. Start watering when the flower stem or leaves start to appear, and water sparingly – only when the compost starts to dry out. Nerines like plenty of sun and airy conditions. Liquid feed the bulbs when they are in full growth. Cease watering when the leaves start dying down to give the bulbs a rest, and resume in late summer or early autumn. Every three years re-pot.

SINNINGIA   Gloxinia

Temperature: 15.5°C (60°F).

Characteristics: Gloxinias are tuberous plants, hybrids of *Sinningia speciosa*, and produce their large bell-shaped blooms in summer, in shades of red, pink, purple and white, including bi-colours.

Cultivation: The tubers are potted in early spring, one per 12.5 cm (5 in) pot, with the tops only just below the surface of the compost. A temperature of 18–21°C (65–70°F) is needed to start them into growth, which could be provided with an electrically heated propagating case.

Water moderately during the growing season and liquid feed fortnightly. High humidity is recommended and shade from strong sunshine. The tubers are dried off in the autumn and stored in frost-free conditions for the winter.

SPREKELIA

Temperature: 10°C (50°F).

Characteristics: The Mexican *Sprekelia formosissima* is a summer-flowering bulb with crimson orchid-like blooms.

Cultivation: In late winter pot the bulb in a 12.5 cm (5 in) pot of soil-based compost, making sure the neck is exposed above compost level. At first give very little water, but gradually increase as growth develops. Good light is needed but shade from the hottest sun and give adequate ventilation. In autumn dry off the bulb and store for the winter in its pot in frost-free conditions.

TULIPS

Temperature: Suitable for cool or unheated conservatory.

Characteristics: All kinds of tulips make good pot plants for flowering in winter or spring in the unheated or cool conservatory. The specially prepared bulbs for Christmas flowering need more warmth, however.

Cultivation: This is the same as for hyacinths and planting time is early autumn.

VALLOTA   Scarborough lily

Temperature: 7°C (45°F)

Characteristics: The South African *Vallota speciosa* is a summer or autumn-flowering bulb with large funnel-shaped scarlet blooms.

Cultivation: Pot the bulb in late summer using a 12.5 cm (5 in) pot of soil-based compost. The neck should be exposed. Apply very little water to start with, but increase as growth develops. The leaves will start to die down in late spring or early summer, an indication to dry off the bulb and give it a rest. Repot only every three years. Start into growth again in late summer.

ZANTEDESCHIA   Arum lily

Temperature: 10°C (50°F).

Characteristics: *Zantedeschia aethiopica* is a popular South African plant which grows from a fleshy rhizome and produces in summer white flowers consisting of a large spathe and spadix. There are several other species of arum lily including the yellow *Z. elliottiana* from the Transvaal, and the pink *Z. rehmannii* from Natal. Zantedeschias from New Zealand with coloured spathes are now available and come in gold, yellow, orange-red, pale and deep pink and bright red.

Cultivation: Plants can be potted in early spring and started into growth. Do not apply too much water at first but increase as growth gets underway. In the summer feed fortnightly with liquid fertilizer. Arum lilies are dried off in the autumn to give them a rest; *Z. aethiopica* should not be treated in this way but kept moist all year round.

Good use is being made of the space under the staging in this warm conservatory. The lush green growth is that of tropical ferns. On the staging are many desirable foliage plants, like the silvery *Fittonia argyroneura*, the purple-spotted maranta in the foreground, as well as *Ficus benjamina*, dizygotheca, peperomias, *Rhoeo discolor minima*, and *Pseuderanthemum reticulatum*.

Aquatics

CYPERUS Umbrella grass

Temperature: 13°C (55°F).
Characteristics: *Cyperus alternifolius* grows to about 60 cm (2 ft) in height and has stiff green stems, at the top of which radiate green leafy bracts, rather like the ribs of an umbrella. The variety 'Variegatus' is striped white and green.
Cultivation: Grow in the shallow water at the edge of a pool. Plant in pure loam in a plastic openwork aquatic basket, in mid-or late spring.

EICHHORNIA Water hyacinth

Temperature: Ideal water temperature 18–21°C (65–70°F), minimum 13°C (55°F).
Characteristics: The water hyacinth is a vigorous grower with rosettes of shiny leaves and pale blue flowers. It comes from tropical America and is correctly know as *Eichhornia crassipes*.
Cultivation: This is a floating aquatic, so simply drop the plant in the water.

NELUMBO Sacred lotus

Temperature: 13°C (55°F)
Characteristics: *Nelumbo nucifera* is rather similar to a waterlily, having large leaves and rose-pink flowers. It is a vigorous plant and needs a large pool, or it can be grown on its own in a large tub.
Cultivation: It is grown in the same way as nymphaea (see below), and needs the same temperatures.

NYMPHAEA Tropical waterlilies

Temperature: 13°C (55°F)
Characteristics: The tropical waterlilies are not difficult to grow provided you maintain the recommended temperatures. For small pools or large tubs, some of the blue-flowered species are suitable, including *Nymphaea caerulea* with scented blooms, and *N. stellata*. There are numerous hybrid waterlilies and these need a reasonably large pool – at least 1.8 by 1.2 m (6 × 4 ft), and preferably larger.

Try one of the following: 'General Pershing', pink, scented flowers; the blue 'Henry Shaw'; 'Missouri', white flowers which open at night; and the yellow 'St. Louis'.
Cultivation: In late winter or early spring each year the tubers are started into growth. Pot these singly into 10 cm (4 in) pots of pure loam and slightly submerge them in a container of water. A temperature of 18–21°C (65–70°C) is needed, so ideally place them in an electrically heated propagating case.

When the tubers start to form leaves, plant each tuber in a large aquatic basket, using loam. Cover the surface with shingle, then place in the pool. Do not put waterlillies straight into deep water, though, but lower them gradually as the leaf stalks grow. This is easily done by standing the baskets on bricks, and removing them as growth increases. To start with there should be no more than 15 cm (6 in) of water over the baskets. A minimum water temperature of 18°C (65°F) is required.

In the autumn the baskets are lifted out of the pool and the soil allowed to dry out. When the leaves have died back, lift the tubers and place them in moist sand. Overwinter in a temperature of 13°C (55°F).

PISTIA Water lettuce

Temperature: 18°C (65°F)
Characterstics: *Pistia stratiotes* is a floating aquatic with rosettes of pale green leaves. It comes from the tropics.
Cultivation: As this is a floating aquatic simply drop the plant into the water.

ZANTEDESCHIA Arum lily

Temperature: 10°C (50°F)
Characteristics: See entry under Bulbous and Tuberous Plants. It can be grown in the shallow water at the edge of a pool.
Cultivation: Plant in an aquatic basket, using pure loam, in the spring. Cover surface of loam with shingle. Place the basket so that there is only a few inches of water over the soil surface.

Summer colour in a temperate conservatory provided by pink and purple streptocarpus hybrids. The tall orange-flowered plant is *Kohleria eriantha*, and the plants with white blooms in the background are *Whitfieldia elongata*. The ivy (*Hedera helix* 'Goldheart') is being grown as a column, and the edge of the staging is softened with the trailing *Callisia repens*, with variegated foliage.

Submerged Oxygenating Plants

These are the so-called water weeds which grow under water, giving off essential oxygen. They ensure a well-aerated pool and clear water. Choose the right kinds (available from aquatic specialists) for the conditions you are able to provide. For instance, there is *Cryptocoryne* which needs warm water; *Myriophyllum* species, some of which will thrive in cool water, and others in warm; and *Vallisneria* species, again for cool or warm conditions. All of these can be planted in loam in aquatic baskets, which should then be placed in the bottom of the pool. A good time for planting is mid- or late spring.

Fruits

CITRUS FRUITS   Oranges and lemons

Temperature: 7–10°C (45–50°F).
Characteristics: Oranges, lemons and even grapefruits make excellent tub plants for the conservatory and given sufficiently high temperatures will bear fruits. All are evergreen spiny shrubs and trees from eastern Asia and produce fragrant flowers in spring or summer. Even if they do not fruit due to lack of heat, they make fine foliage plants.

Among the oranges available are *Citrus aurantium,* the Seville or sour orange; *C. mitis,* the Calamondin, a 45 cm (18 in) high ornamental species which freely produces its tiny fruits; *C. reticulata,* the Mandarin or tangerine; and *C. sinensis,* the sweet orange, of which there are many varieties, these being the oranges we buy in the shops.

The lemon is *C. limon,* and the grapefruit *C. × paradisi,* which is also well worth trying to obtain. In tubs all of these species, with the exception of *C. mitis,* will attain a height of at least 1.2 m (4 ft) although they are capable of growing taller.

Cultivation: Young plants should be potted on until they are eventually in large pots or tubs. Use soil-based potting compost. Pot on during the winter. Plants in final containers

should be top dressed annually in spring with a mixture of loam and well-rotted manure, first removing about 5 cm (2 in) of the old compost.

In winter keep the compost only just moist and provide the minimum temperature. In spring and summer water freely, spray the foliage in warm weather and provide light shade. Very airy conditions are also needed, and indeed the plants can with advantage be stood out of doors from early summer until early autumn. Choose a position in full sun and if possible plunge the pots or tubs in well-weathered ashes to prevent rapid drying out. To encourage the plants to mature their fruit, a temperature of 18–24°C (65–75°F) is needed in the growing period.

Citrus do not require regular pruning but, in order to keep the plants shapely, light pruning can be carried out every two or three years. Shoots can be shortened by up to two-thirds. This shaping should be carried out in early spring. Citrus are very prone to infestations of scale insects and these should be kept under control.

VITIS VINIFERA   Grape vine

Temperature: Little or no heat needed in winter during the rest period.
Characteristics: The grape vine is the traditional conservatory fruit although when trained by the traditional method needs a fair amount of space and therefore is really only suitable for the medium-sized to large conservatory.

The most popular variety is 'Black Hamburgh' with black fruits, suitable for an unheated or slightly heated conservatory. If you prefer white grapes I can recommend 'Buckland Sweetwater', also suitable for an unheated or slightly heated conservatory. Needing the same conditions is 'Foster's Seedling', also a white grape. If you can provide a steady minimum of 15.5°C (60°F) in the spring, and in autumn when fruits are ripening, you might like to grow the luscious, white-fruited 'Muscat of Alexandria'.
Cultivation: Traditionally a grape vine is

An inside view of the conservatory designed and built by Norman and Tina Ellis (p.52).
The conservatory is south facing and, as can be seen, a grape vine, trained up into the
roof, flourishes here.

grown on the back wall of the conservatory and the rod (the main stem) trained up the wall and into the roof area.

Start by planting a young vine in the winter in a well-drained soil bed or border. Ideally the soil should consist of good-quality loam with some well-rotted manure mixed in. If your soil is naturally poor it is a good idea to buy in some good loam or topsoil specially for the vine. Dig out the existing soil to a depth of about 6o cm (2 ft) and fill up with loam.

If you are growing more than one vine allow 1.2 m (4 ft) between them. The rod should be pruned back to a height of 6o cm (2 ft) above soil level after planting.

The rod is trained to a system of horizontal wires, spaced 3o cm (12 in) apart up the wall and into the roof area. Select one strong new shoot in the spring and train it up the wires, removing any other shoots produced.

Side shoots will be produced from this rod, and when they are 6o cm (2 ft) long cut out the tips to prevent further growth. Then in the following winter they are pruned back to within one growth bud of their base. The length of the main rod may also need reducing, so again in winter cut it back to well-ripened wood.

Coming now to the second year, the new side shoots produced in spring are trained horizontally to the wires. You may allow one or two to carry fruits in the second year, but remove most bunches to allow the vine to become well established. These side shoots will need stopping at two leaves beyond a bunch of fruits or they will grow exceedingly long. In the second and subsequent years winter pruning consists of cutting back all side shoots to within one or two growth buds of their base.

The main rod should be untied in late winter and lowered to a horizontal position, supporting it with string attached to a roof wire. This will ensure that shoots break evenly all along the length of the rod. When shoots are being produced, re tie the rod to its normal vertical position.

Let us now consider routine management of the grape vine. After the second year, one can allow two or three bunches of grapes to develop on each side shoot. In order to secure fruits, the flowers will need to be hand pollinated. All you do here is to draw your half-closed hand gently down each truss of flowers when they are fully open. The atmosphere should be dry during this task.

Many berries will be produced in each bunch and they must be thinned out otherwise they will not have sufficient space to develop. Thinning is done with a pair of fine-tipped vine scissors. Do not touch the berries with your hands or you will remove the waxy 'bloom'. Instead, during thinning steady the bunch with a thin, forked stick. As soon as the berries are the size of peas thin out the centre of each bunch. Further thinning will be necessary as the fruits swell – the aim being to leave each one sufficient space to develop to its full size.

Cut out the side shoots at two leaves beyond a bunch of fruits. These side shoots will produce shoots themselves (known as sub-laterals) and these should be cut back to one leaf.

Very good ventilation is needed to prevent vine mildew. It is not necessary to provide artificial heat in the winter when the vines are resting but if possible provide heat in the spring when the vine is in flower. One relies on natural warmth in summer and autumn, when a minimum temperature of 13°C (55°F) is needed.

In warm conditions, damp down the conservatory to provide a humid atmosphere. However, the air should be dry when the vine is in flower and when the fruits are ripening. Water freely when the vine is in full growth but keep the soil only slightly moist when the plant is resting in the winter. Feeding is recommended in the summer: it is possible to buy a special vine fertilizer, otherwise use a general-purpose type. You will probably have to buy a vine fertilizer from a specialist fertilizer supplier, as it is not usually available from garden centres.

PRUNUS PERSICA   Peaches and nectarines

Temperature: Best to have no artificial heat in winter when plants are resting.

Characteristics: It is not difficult to produce luscious peaches and nectarines in a conservatory for they are hardy plants needing minimum artificial heat. I have grouped both the fruits together for they are grown in exactly the same way, and in fact the

I would advise buying a two-year-old fan-trained tree. You will probably need to buy from a specialist fruit grower. Planting time is late autumn or winter.

The newly planted tree is pruned very hard – the middle branch (which is growing vertically) is cut right back to the topmost side branches. The two lowest side branches should then be cut back lightly and tied in to one of the horizontal wires. All pruning cuts

Fig. 7. Peaches (*left*) and nectarines (*right*).

nectarine is simply a smooth-skinned form of peach.

There are several varieties of peach available including 'Bellegarde', 'Dymond', 'Hale's Early', 'Peregrin' and 'Royal George'. Nectarine varieties include 'Early Rivers', 'Lord Napier' and 'Pine Apple'.

Cultivation: Peaches and nectarines can be trained to the shape of a fan on the back wall of the conservatory. For each tree you will need wall space of at least 1.8 by 1.8 m (6 by 6 ft).

Plant in a well-drained soil bed or border as for grape vines, and put up horizontal wires for training, spaced 20 cm (8 in) apart.

should be made just above dormant growth buds. Growth buds on peaches and nectarines are the long thin ones, whereas flower buds are fat and rounded in shape. Any remaining branches should now be pruned back to within a few centimetres of the main stem.

In the spring after this pruning many new shoots will be produced. They must be thinned out to avoid congestion. When carried out early enough, they can simply be rubbed out with the fingers. The aim is to leave only sufficient new shoots to form a fan-shaped system of main branches. As these shoots grow tie them in to the wires, spacing them out as evenly as possible to form a neat fan shape. Never leave on the plant any shoots which are growing outwards. Shoots growing sideways, upwards or downwards are the ones to train.

We now come to the second winter. By this time the main branches should have produced several shoots along their length and made extension growth. You may find that some of the shoots have produced flower buds, and you can allow a few fruits to develop. The shoots should be tied in as flat as possible to the wires.

This is the basic method of training, but peaches and nectarines should be pruned annually in winter. Shoots which have carried fruits (and which are produced on the main framework of branches) are pruned back to new shoots. These replace the ones cut back and will carry fruits in the following summer. Therefore, there is a constant succession of fruiting shoots.

Now to general care other than pruning. The trees will rest between late autumn and late winter and need little or no artificial heat. However, very airy conditions are required, so ventilate well whenever the weather is fine.

The buds will start to swell in the spring, a sign to reduce ventilation and to give a little artificial heat, maintaining, say, a temperature of 7°C (45°F), especially when the trees are in flower. During mild spells spray the trees with plain water twice a day. Damp down the floor in warm spells.

The flowers need to be hand pollinated to secure fruits, for there are no pollinating insects around early in the year. I use a soft paintbrush (the type used by artists), simply dabbing the centre of each flower in turn to distribute the pollen from one to another.

In the spring the trees will produce many new shoots and these should be thinned out to avoid congestion. You should leave sufficient at the base of the flowering/fruiting ones for fruiting next year and remove the rest.

The fruitlets will need thinning, too; leave two or three on each shoot, making sure they are evenly spaced. In the summer provide airy conditions, spray the trees twice a day with plain water, and damp down the floor once or twice a day. Fruit and shoot thinning should continue as necessary. I feed the trees with a high-potash fertilizer in the summer, using a dry fertilizer as a topdressing, pricking it into the surface of the soil. The fertilizer can be watered in.

When the fruits are ripening you should cease spraying, stop watering the soil, and give as much ventilation as possible. After harvesting the fruits, resume watering and spraying. When leaf fall occurs, stop spraying. From now on reduce watering, applying only sufficient to keep the soil slightly moist.

7
CHOOSING PLANTS FOR LIVING AREAS

As I see the situation, having talked to many people in recent years, a conservatory is purchased for one of two distinct reasons: primarily for growing plants, or mainly to provide living space for the owners.

In the first instance, where the prime consideration is growing plants, the conservatory owner is not faced with problems, for he or she will maintain an environment which is suited to the plants, but not necessarily to humans. He or she will be content to spend only comparatively short periods in the conservatory, tending and admiring the plants, and the unsuitable atmosphere (for humans, that is) will not be a problem. In a plant conservatory a warm steamy 'jungle' atmosphere might be maintained, or very cool conditions in winter for plants which do not like too much heat.

However, where the conservatory is required for living in, the atmosphere must be suited to humans. Few people would want to work, play, relax, eat or entertain friends in an atmosphere reminiscent of a South American 'jungle', or at the other extreme wrapped up in winter clothing. Unfortunately, the atmosphere required by humans is not suited to a great many plants, so plants must be chosen with care, or cared for extra well if they are to survive. In a conservatory used for living in, plants are generally regarded as part of the decoration and furnishing schemes, in much the same way as houseplants are used. Quite possibly in a living area, therefore, plants would be used sparingly, the furniture playing a dominant part in the overall scheme of things.

For instance, one might have a large specimen plant or two in a corner to provide a dramatic feature, and perhaps groups of smaller plants on a table or in 'planters' on the floor. A few hanging containers of trailing plants might also be used, or a climbing plant might be trained to ornamental wall trellis or be free standing, trained perhaps to a tall moss pole.

The ideal living area

The ideal atmosphere to maintain in a conservatory used for living in is not easy to describe, for really it depends on the preferences of the owners. Only you know what is a comfortable temperature to maintain all year round.

However most people would maintain a steady temperature between 15·5 and 21°C (60 and 70°F). As with the rest of the house this would mean providing artificial heat in the autumn, winter and spring.

Such a temperature would be ideal for many plants, too, especially those of tropical and sub-tropical origin. For comfort, the level of atmospheric humidity should be low and indeed living areas generally have a dry atmosphere. One cannot live comfortably in an area of high humidity. Unfortunately, most plants do not like a combination of high temperatures and dry air. Tropical and sub-tropical plants, for instance, would make very poor growth and the leaves may shrivel and dry up, or turn brown at the edges. However, there are ways of ensuring plants have sufficient humidity without a moisture-laden atmosphere. And of course there are plants that actually thrive in warm, dry conditions. More about these later.

Now to the subject of light and shade. A conservatory must be fitted with blinds which can be rolled down in sunny weather, not only to reduce the glare of the sun, but also to help keep the temperature down in warm weather. A conservatory is like a greenhouse, of course: as soon as the sun shines the temperature rises, for the heat is trapped in the structure.

There is no problem with shade as far as plants are concerned for they, like humans, need shade from the sun and indeed would suffer if not protected. Many tropical and sub-tropical plants naturally inhabit shady places, such as forest floors. Details of blinds of various kinds are given in Chapter 2.

As already indicated, one of the problems in warm weather is trying to keep the temperature down to a comfortable level. Fortunately this is fairly easily achieved as most conservatories are fitted with plenty of ventilators and opening windows. And, of course, the doors can also be left open. Also extractor or circulating fans could be installed. Such ventilation is also ideal for plants, as most need plenty of fresh air in warm weather. Ventilation equipment is recommended in Chapter 2.

These, then, are what I consider to be suitable living conditions. They are almost perfect for a great many plants, except for lack of humidity. So how can we ensure that the plants have sufficient humidity? If you have the time, spray them daily or twice daily with plain water, using a small, house-plant mist sprayer. The moisture evaporating off the leaves will keep plants happy and will not affect the atmosphere.

Alternatively, plants could be stood on trays of gravel or pebbles, or even plunged to the pot rims in these materials. The gravel or pebbles should be kept permanently moist so that humid conditions are created around the plants. You will be providing a 'micro-climate' for the plants, while the atmosphere in the rest of the conservatory will be comfortable for living in. Full details of this technique will be found in Chapter 8.

Choosing plants for the 'lived-in' conservatory

As already indicated there are many plants which can be grown in the 'lived-in' conservatory provided you are able to create a humid 'micro-climate' around them. All of the following can be recommended and as they are extracted from the descriptive lists in Chapter 6, I will omit descriptions of them.

This octagonal-ended timber modular conservatory from Amdega Ltd incorporates a lean-to section, dentil moulding and ridge cresting. Approximate size: 5.4 × 4 m (18 × 13½ ft).

(*Below*) Also from Amdega Ltd, a double-glazed timber conservatory incorporating a link corridor, with extra-high side framing, dentil moulding and ridge cresting. Approximate dimensions: 6.9 × 3.6 m (23 × 12 ft).

Plants which like warm conditions and high humidity:

Shrubs: *Aphelandra, Crossandra, Gardenia, Jacobinia, Nerium* and *Tibouchina.*

Climbers: *Allamanda, Bougainvillea, Clerodendron, Dipladenia, Hoya* and *Stephanotis.*

Flowering pot plants – short term: *Browallia, Capsicum, Celosia, Exacum, Impatiens* and *Solanum.*

Flowering pot plants – long term: *Anthurium, Begonia, Euphorbia pulcherrima, Saintpaulia* and *Streptocarpus.*

Foliage pot plants: *Aglaeonema, Asparagus, Begonia,* Bromeliads, *Calathea, Chlorophytum, Cissus, Codiaeum, Coleus, Cordyline, Ctenanthe, Dieffenbachia, Dracaena,* Ferns, *Ficus, Maranta, Monstera,* Palms, *Peperomia, Philodendron, Scindapsus, Tradescantia* and *Zebrina.*

Bulbous and tuberous plants: *Begonia, Canna* and *Sinningia.*

Fruits: *Citrus.*

Plants which like warm conditions and will thrive in a dry atmosphere:

Shrubs: *Bouvardia, Cestrum* and *Lantana.*

Climbers: *Plumbago.*

Flowering pot plants – short term: *Ipomoea.*

Flowering pot plants – long term: *Fuchsia* and *Pelargoniums.* Cacti and succulents will also thrive in warm, dry conditions.

Foliage pot plants: *Sansevieria.*

Bulbous and tuberous plants: *Gloriosa, Hippeastrum, Sprekelia* and *Vallota.*

Ways of displaying plants

As with plants in the rest of the home, most people would want to display them attractively, and this means hiding the pots, for clay or plastic pots are not the most attractive objects.

There are available all kinds of ornamental pot holders, in which the pots are stood. The space between the pot and the side of the container could with advantage be filled with gravel or peat, which should be kept moist for those subjects which like a humid atmosphere.

Go to any large garden centre and you will find a good range of pot holders. They may be made from plastic, copper, brass, wood or pottery. I have also come across cane and wicker-work pot holders, which look most attractive. However, with porous kinds you will need to place a drip tray or dish in the bottom to catch surplus water. All sizes are available, suitable for the smallest to the largest pot.

I would suggest you go for fairly plain pot holders rather than heavily patterned, as in my opinion the latter detract from the beauty of the plants. However, various colours can be chosen, ideally soft or pastel colours, including buff, beige, cream and pale green. White also looks good, as does black and all shades of brown.

There are many other 'objects' which could be used as pot holders and I particularly like rummaging around antique shops for such things as old brass coal scuttles and copper cooking pots.

For groups of plants there are many large floor containers available, fairly deep so that you can plunge pots to their rims in peat or shingle. These generally come in plastic or wood. When grouping plants together make sure they all need the same conditions in respect of light, temperature and humidity. There is no doubt in my mind that plants grow much better when grouped, as they create their own micro-climate.

If eventually some of your plants grow so large that they need planting in tubs, then again there is a good choice from garden centres. You could buy the large, ornamental terra-cotta tubs, for instance, or you may prefer wooden tubs, suitably stained and varnished. Such containers have drainage holes in the bottom, so they should be stood on a tray to catch surplus water.

For trailing plants there are many attractive hanging containers available; for instance in terra-cotta, or the more conventional hanging baskets. When buying hanging baskets for a living area make sure you choose those kinds which have a built-in drip tray to prevent the floor from becoming wet when watering.

An attractive way to display epiphytic (tree-dwelling) plants, like many of the bromeliads, is on a plant tree, the plants simply being tied on or gently wedged into place. Details of how to make a plant tree will be found in Chapter 4. The only problem with this in a conservatory for living in is that the plants have to be sprayed with water and this may wet the floor. However, it may be possible to stand the tree on a fairly large tray to catch any drips.

To summarize, when growing plants in the 'lived-in' conservatory, think in terms of growing them as houseplants, for essentially this type of conservatory is the same as a living room in the house.

The seasonal living area

If you cannot afford to maintain a comfortable temperature during the colder months of the year – which in the U.K. is usually late autumn, winter and the early part of spring – then the conservatory could be used for living in only between, say, late spring and early autumn.

There is usually sufficient natural warmth during this period of the year, when many people make maximum use of their conservatories; for instance, relaxing with a drink on a warm summer's evening, taking meals and for entertaining friends. In the spring and summer the conservatory is also a pleasant place in which to relax on wet days.

However, if the sun appears in winter the conservatory can become surprisingly warm even at that time of year, for it traps the heat, so do not rule out the occasional 'coffee morning' in the winter amidst pleasant greenery and flowering pot plants.

I am thinking in terms of maintaining a minimum winter temperature of between 4.5° and 10°C (40° to 50°F). This will allow you to grow a good range of plants. With a minimum of 4.5° to 7°C (40° to 45°F), you will be maintaining what is correctly known as a 'cool' conservatory'; and with a minimum of 10°C it will be an 'intermediate conservatory'. With a minimum of 10°C you will be able to grow a much wider range of plants than if you maintain a minimum of 4.5° – 7°C, but you will have to bear in mind that the heating bills will be considerably higher.

These minimum temperatures are not comfortable enough to live in for any length of time, at least I do not find them so. But such conditions are ideal for those plants which like cool conditions.

As far as plants are concerned, you should keep the air dry when conditions are cool, but as the weather warms up in the spring and summer many of the plants will appreciate some humidity, provided as outlined in 'The Ideal Living Area', p.107.

You may want to grow tropical and sub-tropical plants in your conservatory, but of course most will not tolerate the cool conditions in the winter. So between, say, early autumn and late spring they should be kept in a warm room indoors and treated as houseplants. They will certainly benefit from a spell in the conservatory during the summer, and will welcome the better light and perhaps less-stuffy conditions. It is surprising just how much growth many of them make when they have a 'holiday' in the conservatory.

There are many plants, though, that can be grown in the cool or intermediate conservatory all the year round, so you should never be short of attractive greenery and flowers even in the winter. Indeed, there are many pot plants for autumn, winter and spring flowering, and one should not forget, either, the hardy bulbs which bloom in winter and spring. In Chapter 6 I have described many plants suitable for the cool and intermediate conservatory, but for quick reference I have listed them below.

Some of the plants need a minimum temperature of 10°C (50°F), while others will succeed with a minimum of 4.5 – 7°C (40° – 45°F). I have lumped them all together here, so do check minimum temperature requirements in Chapter 6.

Plants for the cool and intermediate conservatory:

Shrubs: *Abutilon, Acacia, Bouvardia, Brunfelsia, Callistemon, Camellia, Cassia, Cestrum, Datura, Erythrina, Hibiscus, Lantana, Nerium, Rhododendron, Sparmannia* and *Tibouchina*.

Climbers: *Bougainvillea, Clianthus, Hoya, Jasminum, Lapageria, Mandevilla, Passiflora* and *Plumbago*.

Flowering pot plants – short-term: Annuals (hardy), *Browallia, Calceolaria, Campanula, Capsicum, Celosia, Chrysanthemum, Impatiens, Ipomoea, Primula, Salpiglossis, Schizanthus, Senecio* and *Solanum.*

Flowering pot plants – long-term: Carnivorous plants, *Clivia, Cymbidium, Erica, Fuchsia, Hydrangea, Pelargonium, Strelitzia* and *Streptocarpus.*

Foliage pot plants: *Asparagus,* Bromeliads, *Chlorophytum, Cissus, Coleus,* Ferns, *Grevillea, Hedera,* Palms, *Sansevieria, Tradescantia* and *Zebrina.*

Bulbous and tuberous plants: *Cyclamen, Freesia, Hippeastrum,* Hyacinths, *Lilium, Narcissus, Nerine, Sprekelia,* Tulips, *Vallota* and *Zantedeschia.*

Fruits: *Citrus, Vitis vinifera* and *Prunus persica.* The last two are really better without heat in the winter, but *very* cool conditions would be acceptable, say, just frost free.

Ways of displaying plants

The advice given under 'The Ideal Living Area' (p.107) equally applies to the cooler conservatory. In cooler conditions you may well have more plants, though, for if it is not to be filled with people in the colder months of the year, it should certainly be filled with plants.

It pays to take a little care over arranging plants to create some pleasing displays. I like grouping plants, flowering and foliage kinds, for maximum effect. A conservatory should not be like a greenhouse where plants are generally arranged in rows or blocks of each variety – it is meant to be a display area.

To give you an idea of what I mean, try arranging foliage plants like asparagus, ferns, grevillea and hederas among spring-flowering bulbs, such as daffodils, hyacinths and tulips.

Such foliage plants also make a superb foil for flowering pot plants, particularly primulas, senecio, calceolarias, capsicums and solanums.

For a summer display I like to arrange variegated abutilons, chlorophytums and coleus with summer-flowering pot plants like fuchsias, pelargoniums, streptocarpus, celosias and impatiens.

Many ideas are to be found in the greenhouses of public parks, botanical gardens and private gardens open to the general public. I always have a notebook handy and jot down any pleasing combinations that I come across.

The unheated conservatory

With the ever-rising cost of heating, many people are finding that they simply cannot afford to heat a conservatory. However, even a 'cold' conservatory, as it is correctly termed, can still be used as a seasonal living area as soon as the weather warms up sufficiently in the spring. You should be able to make good use of the conservatory throughout the summer months and into the autumn.

Of course, the great problem is that you will not be able to keep tender plants in the conservatory over the winter for they will become frosted. Again the solution is to keep them in a warm room indoors over the winter.

You should be able to have a good summer display of such plants as fuchsias, pelargoniums, streptocarpus, celosias, impatiens, and others. In the autumn you could have a fine display of greenhouse chrysanthemums.

The cold conservatory is an ideal place to grow grapes, peaches and nectarines as they do not need heat in the winter.

But having ensured summer and autumn colour and interest, we now need to consider how to keep the conservatory interesting and colourful during the winter and spring. It is, of course, a case of furnishing it with hardy plants.

Camellias are an excellent choice for the unheated conservatory, growing them in tubs and keeping them out of doors for the summer. Depending on variety, they will flower in winter and spring. The hardy annuals grown in pots will flower in the spring in an unheated conservatory and a superb display they make, too. Sadly, they are not often grown by amateur gardeners for this purpose, yet they are so easy.

Hardy bulbs will flower in spring – hyacinths, narcissus and tulips, and their blooms should be perfect as they will be well protected from the weather.

I like to grow the hardy winter-flowering heathers in pots and to take them into the conservatory as they are coming into flower. There are many varieties of *Erica carnea,* like 'Springwood Pink', 'Springwood White' and 'Winter Beauty' ('King George'). They are neat, low-growing, compact plants and look particularly good when arranged with some dwarf conifers in pots. Conifers provide attractive foliage for the winter but during the warmer months should be kept out of doors.

There are plenty of hardy foliage plants which could be grown in pots and taken into the cold conservatory for the winter. I am particularly fond of *Fatsia japonica,* an evergreen shrub with huge hand-shaped glossy green leaves. Eventually it makes quite a large specimen, so if it becomes too big you could either plant it out in the garden or grow it in a large tub, provided you are able to move it.

Also, why not consider growing a hardy palm in a pot or tub to give an exotic touch to the winter conservatory? Again this could be moved outside if desired for the summer. The one to grow is the Chusan palm, *Trachycarpus fortunei,* which forms a tall fibrous-coated trunk at the top of which is a cluster of typical palm leaves. Eventually it may flower, producing panicles of many small yellow blooms.

Also palm-like in appearance is the cabbage tree, *Cordyline australis.* Again this can be pot grown and kept out of doors for the summer. This produces a single trunk with thick upward-growing branches and dramatic sword-like leaves, giving a decidedly exotic touch to the cold conservatory. There is also a variety available with purple leaves called 'Atropurpurea'.

Alexander Bartholomew Conservatories Ltd are specialists in timber double-glazed conservatories and can provide every shape and size to suit customers' requirements. This unusual, elevated conservatory is one of their designs.

One should not forget the many ivies, for trailing over the edge of the staging, for hanging containers or for growing as climbers up canes, wire hoops, etc. These are described in Chapter 6. In cold conditions you may find that the foliage of some of them changes colour, perhaps taking on reddish or purplish tints – this is quite normal.

To my mind among the best plants for flowering in the cold conservatory during winter and spring are the alpines, like saxifrages, alpine primulas and spring-flowering gentians. These are grown in pans of gritty soil-based compost and taken into the conservatory as they are coming into flower. For the rest of the year they can be kept in a well-ventilated cold frame.

Good companions for alpines are the various dwarf and miniature hardy bulbs, like crocus species, especially *Crocus chrysanthus* varieties, chionodoxas, miniature cyclamen, galanthus or snowdrops, miniature irises, muscari, miniature narcissus species, scillas, and dwarf tulip species. These, too, can be grown in pans and taken into the conservatory in the autumn. For the rest of the year, after flowering, keep them in a cold frame.

To complete the display of alpines and dwarf bulbs, arrange among them some dwarf conifers in pots such as *Picea albertiana* 'Conica', *Juniperus communis* 'Compressa' and *Pinus parviflora brevifolia*.

When temperatures are low in the autumn and winter, and into spring, you must keep the atmosphere as dry as possible in the cold conservatory. Do not splash water around, water plants with care to keep them only moderately moist, and above all provide plenty of ventilaton, except during gales or fog. Dry airy conditions will ensure your plants thrive instead of rotting off.

The non-living area

So far I have been considering the conservatory which can be lived in for all or part of the year, and matching the plants' requirements with those of humans. But there is one type of environment sometimes created which is definitely not suitable for living in. This is the very warm or tropical conservatory with high humidity all the year round.

This is strictly for the 'plantsman', the person who enjoys growing tropical plants. Such a conservatory is reminiscent of the Victorian era when plants were grown in so-called 'stove houses', and very exciting it can be, too, if you can afford to maintain an all-year round temperature of at least 18 – 21°C (65 – 70°F). It is not the temperature which is unsuitable for people but the high humidity, reminiscent of a 'steamy' South American 'jungle'.

Needless to say a very wide range of tropical plants can be grown in such conditions, including not only those listed in this book, but also subjects like the pitcher plants, *Nepenthes* species, which are mainly climbers, producing pendent lidded pitches which trap insects and other small creatures. Tropical orchids could also be grown, many of these coming from tropical rain forest where conditions are warm and humid.

Other desirable plants, not mentioned so far in this book, include caladiums with flamboyant multi-coloured leaves; the coloured-leaved acalyphas; tropical ferns, including tree ferns like *Cyathea* species; episcias; *Aeschynanthus; Medinilla magnifica* with sumptuous pink flowers; and selaginellas, grown for their ferny foliage.

The tropical conservatory has to be carefully managed, of course, and the temperature must not be allowed to drop below the minimum level. Higher temperatures during the day should be the aim, and to help achieve this one should give far less ventilation then in a conservatory used for living in. Some ventilation is needed, though, sufficient to prevent stagnant conditions. Even these plants like fresh air.

Many of the plants grown in the tropical conservatory are shade-loving and therefore a good system of roller blinds is needed. These should be fully automatic if you are away all day, so that plants can be shaded during periods of bright sunshine.

High humidity is essential and this means damping down the conservatory floor and the staging at least once a day and preferably twice – morning and evening. During very warm conditions the plants should also be sprayed with plain water once or twice a day.

Enjoy your conservatory

Hopefully, I have outlined ideas to suit all conservatory owners; at least I have considered all the possibilities. The main thing is to enjoy to the full the conditions it provides for here you have a completely different environment to the other rooms in the house. In my opinion, being a plantsman and gardener, a conservatory is a far better choice than the normal room extension when extra space is needed for living. Moreover, it adds far more character to a house if carefully chosen and furnished.

8
CARING FOR THE PLANTS

To ensure your plants flourish, lavish care and attention on them and make sure the basic techniques of watering, feeding, potting, pruning and so on are carried out correctly. Here is a basic guide to routine plant care throughout the year.

Watering

This aspect of plant care causes more problems with the newcomer to gardening than any other. He or she is often uncertain of when to water plants and how much water to apply. Yet this technique has to be mastered, for if plants are kept too wet they are liable to suffer root rot and eventually they die. If plants are given insufficient water they will be under considerable stress and will not grow and flower well.

You will find that I have indicated in Chapter 6 water requirements for the plants. Generally, although it does not apply to all plants, more water is needed in the growing period (spring and summer for most) than in the rest period (autumn and winter).

Let us, therefore, start with ascertaining when to water plants in the growing period. Bear in mind that with most subjects we do not want the compost to dry out too much during this period. I would advise testing the compost or soil for moisture with a finger. Press a finger into the surface and if it feels dry on top, but moist below, then apply water. If the surface is moist or even wet, do not water. When watering do not give a 'quick splash', but fill the space between the compost surface and the rim of the pot with water. This will ensure the compost is moistened right the way down to the bottom of the pot.

The soil in a bed or border can be tested in the same way: apply sufficient water to penetrate to a depth of about 15 cm (6 in), which means giving about 27 litres/square metre (4¾ gallons/square yard).

When watering in the autumn and winter, during the plants' rest period, and when conditions are cooler, I have advised in Chapter 6 to keep the compost or soil only slightly moist, to water more sparingly or to reduce watering for many of the plants. How can we put this into practice? Again I would adivse testing with a finger, pushing it well down into the compost. If the compost is dry on the surface, and feels dryish but not completely dry lower down, water can be applied, again filling the space between the compost surface and the rim of the pot. Then leave well alone until the compost is drying out again. It is far better not to water if in doubt, than to keep the compost too wet. Far better to leave the plant for a few more days, unless it is wilting.

Feeding

Potting composts supply plants with foods for a certain period, generally several months, depending on the type of fertilizer used in the mix. Therefore newly potted plants do not need feeding. The time to start is when the roots have permeated the new compost which, in practical terms, is about two months. The same applies to plants which have been potted on to larger pots.

Then feeding can be carried out about once a fortnight for most subjects, but only in the growing season – spring and summer – and perhaps early autumn if plants are still making growth. Do not feed in late autumn, winter and early spring, when most plants are resting, for they will not use the fertilizer and an excess of foods can build up in the compost, which can be harmful.

There are various ways of feeding potted plants, but the most popular is to apply a liquid fertilizer. There are many proprietary brands available, but for conservatory plants I would suggest using a houseplant fertilizer. Some of these are based on seaweed.

Another way of feeding potted plants is to use fertilizer tablets, again specially formulated for houseplants. These are about the size of an asprin tablet and are simply pushed into the compost, where they release plant foods over a period of weeks.

There are various ways, too, of feeding permanent plants in soil beds or borders. I like to apply a dry general-purpose fertilizer in mid-spring and lightly prick it into the soil surface. Then in the summer, if I feel that plants need a boost, I water them with a general-purpose liquid fertilizer, say about once a month. Plants in soil beds do not need regular feeding as with potted plants, as foods are not leached out so rapidly.

Plants should not be fed if the compost or soil is dry – water it first and then feed when the plants are fully charged with water.

It is most important to apply fertilizers strictly according to the instructions on the packet or bottle, for you could harm plants by applying too much, or too strong a solution.

Damping down

I have emphasised throughout the book that many plants need a humid atmosphere, particularly in warm conditions. The lower the temperature the drier the air must be. The technique known as damping down provides atmospheric humidity and involves sprinkling the floor and staging with water – perhaps twice a day in very warm conditions, morning and evening.

However, damping down is not a practical proposition for conservatories which are used for living in, for not only does it create too much humidity for comfort, but you may not want to wet the floor. So it is usually reserved for conservatories which are used for the cultivation of plants.

However, plants in living areas still need humidity, but it can be localized. For instance, potted plants could be stood on shallow trays filled with gravel, shingle or one of the horticultural aggregates. These materials are kept moist to create a humid atmosphere around the plants, but make sure the pots do not stand in water or the compost will become too wet.

Another method is to plunge pots to their rims in peat, shingle or horticultural aggregate and to keep these moist. In this instance you will, of course, need deep containers or 'planters'.

Another method of ensuring humid conditions around plants is to spray them daily or twice daily in warm conditions with plain water. Use a small mist sprayer for this – the type designed for indoor use. It is best, though, not to spray flowers, and never spray plants with hairy or woolly leaves, or cacti and succulents. Use soft water or rainwater for spraying plants, for 'hard' or alkaline water can result in unsightly white marks on the leaves.

Ventilating

Plants as well as people need fresh air at all times and therefore adequate ventilation is needed all the year around. Ventilation also helps to reduce the temperature, particularly necessary in hot weather; and it helps to reduce humidity, which is important for plants growing in cold or cool conditions.

The amount of ventilation you provide should be consistent with maintaining the desired temperature – there is no point in providing a great deal of ventilation if it results in the temperature dropping to an uncomfortable level for plants and people.

The way to ensure effective ventilation is to open the roof ventilators and also the side ventilators or louvres. The warm air rises and escapes through the roof, sucking in cool. air through the side ventilators.

Shading

Again adequate shading is needed by both plants and people in the spring and summer. Without shading the leaves and flowers of plants can be badly scorched during periods of strong sunshine. Shading also helps to keep temperatures down to an acceptable level in hot weather.

For plants, shading should ideally only be used when the sun is shining and removed during dull periods so that they receive maximum light, and this is best achieved by the use of roller blinds (see Chapter 2).

As you will have seen in Chapter 6, plants vary in the amount of light or shade needed. Some like plenty of sun, including many cacti and succulents, while others should be well shaded from strong sunshine, includin ferns and many of the tropical plants. For the sake of convenience it would perhaps be better to grow in your conservatory only plants which need to be shaded – that is, if it is used as a living area.

Remember that in autumn and winter plants need all the light they can get, so shading should not be used during these seasons – and I doubt if you will need it either.

Breakfast in the conservatory on a spring morning in Connecticut, U.S.A. The conservatory is Machin Designs V4 Series, size 3.9 × 3.9 m (13 × 13 ft); note the distinctive curved roof of a Machin conservatory.

(*Below*) An excellent example of a Room Outside Ltd. conservatory in complete harmony with the house. It is difficult to believe that the conservatory is a new addition. Approximate dimensions: 4.8 × 3.6 m (16 × 12 ft).

Potting

Most plants make much better growth if they are potted on regularly into larger pots. If allowed to become pot-bound, when the compost is tightly packed with roots, growth will slow down considerably. Also, the compost will dry out very rapidly so you will be forever watering, and there is the risk plants will suffer stress from lack of moisture.

Having said this, there are some plants that should not be potted on regularly, either because they do not like root disturbance or because they have only a small root system; therefore small pots are adequate for their needs. I have indicated this where applicable in Chapter 6.

Try to avoid potting on in winter when plants are resting, for they will not make new roots into the fresh compost and consequently the compost may remain too wet. The roots may then rot.

To ascertain whether or not a plant needs potting on, you will need to inspect the roots. To do this, turn the pot upside down and tap the rim on the edge of a table or bench to loosen the rootball, and slide off the pot. If there is a mass of roots then pot on; but if a large volume of the compost has no roots through it, return the plant to its present pot.

If possible pot on into the next size of pot, for example from a 12.5 cm (5 in) pot to a 15 cm (6 in) pot. However, more vigorous plants can with advantage be moved on two sizes – for instance, from a 10 cm (4 in) pot to a 15 cm (6 in) pot.

The trend these days is to dispense with drainage material in he bottom of the pot. But I feel that for plants which like very well drained conditions drainage material should be provided; and I also think it is necessary when we come onto larger pots – say over 15 cm (6 in) in diameter. The traditional drainage material is broken clay flower pots, known as 'crocks'. A large piece is placed over the drainage hole and then a layer of smaller pieces placed over this. Cover with a thin layer of rough peat or leafmould, followed by a layer of compost which should be firmed. Place the plant in the centre and fill in with compost, firming all round with your fingers. You should ensure the top of the rootball is slightly covered with fresh compost, and there must be space between the final compost level and the rim of the pot to allow room for watering. This can be about 12 mm (½ in) for small pots and up to 2.5 cm (1 in) for larger pots.

After potting water in the plant with a rosed watering can to settle the compost around the roots.

Plastic pots are often used today, but for plants which like very well drained conditions and dryish compost, I prefer clay pots. I also use clay pots for larger plants as they are heavier and more stable.

Now let us take a look at suitable potting composts. You will see in Chapter 6 that some plants are best in soil-based compost, this being the traditional John Innes potting compost, which is well drained and aerated. It is readily available from garden centres and consists of loam (soil), peat and sand, plus John Innes base fertilizer and chalk. John Innes potting compost No. 1 is used for the initial potting of young plants, such as seedlings and rooted cuttings. When potting on use JIP2 which contains twice the amount of fertilizer. When potting on large plants – for instance, shrubs which are being grown in large pots or tubs, use JIP3 which contains three times the amount of fertilizer.

Other plants are happy in the more modern soilless or peat-based composts and again I have indicated this where appropriate in Chapter 6. These consist of peat with fertilizers added, or peat and other materials such as Perlite, plus fertilizers. They are ideal for plants which like plenty of humus and moist conditions, for peat-based composts are inclined to hold more moisture than soil-based types. One needs to be careful to prevent keeping all-peat composts too wet.

There are peat-based composts specially formulated for houseplants and these would be suitable for conservatory plants, too. General-purpose soilless composts would also be suitable. You will find a good range in garden centres.

Planting

Most plants are supplied in pots or some other kind of container such as black polythene 'bags', and therefore can be planted in soil beds and borders at any time of year. But possibly the best time to plant is in late winter or early spring just before the plants start into growth.

The soil bed should have been well prepared before planting, by digging deeply and adding organic matter such as peat, leafmould, well-rotted farmyard manure or garden compost. It should be allowed to settle and then firmed by treading.

Take out a planting hole larger than the rootball of the plant and work some proprietary planting mixture into the soil in the bottom. This is basically peat with fertilizers, specially formulated for shrubs, climbers and so on. Carefully remove the plant from its container to avoid disturbing the roots and place it centrally in the hole, making sure the top of the rootball is slightly below the surrounding soil level – say about 12 mm (½ in). Then return fine soil, to which has been added some planting mixture, around the rootball, firming it as you proceed, with your hands for small plants and with a heel for large specimens.

After planting water well in to settle the soil around the roots. I like to mulch the soil after planting as this not only helps to conserve soil moisture but, if suitable materials are used, provides an attractive finish. One of the most attractive materials is pulverized or shredded bark. Peat is also attractive. Spread a 5 cm (2 in) deep layer over the entire soil surface. The soil must be moist before you apply a mulch.

Pruning

I have indicated how to prune plants where applicable in Chapter 6, so here I will consider only the basic rules.

Firstly, always use really sharp secateurs for it is essential to make clean cuts. These heal very much quicker and better than ragged cuts made with blunt secateurs and are therefore less liable to be infected by diseases.

When you are cutting back branches or shoots, always cut just above a growth bud; not so far above that you leave a portion of stem, which will only die back to the bud, and not so close that you damage the bud, which may not then come into growth. Growth buds are situated in the axil formed between the base of a leaf stalk and the stem.

If you have to remove large branches from say, a shrub, all pruning cuts over 2.5 cm (1 in) in diameter should be 'painted' with a proprietary pruning compound to seal them and prevent the possible entry of diseases. Many plants do not need regular pruning, but you should always keep an eye open for any dead or dying shoots and cut these back to live wood.

Removal of dead flowers is a form of pruning and is certainly recommended, not only for the sake of tidiness but to prevent the disease greymould or botrytis from infecting the dead flowers, from where it could spread to healthy tissue.

Another form of pruning is the technique known as 'stopping' or 'pinching'. This is where the growing tip of a young plant is pinched out or cut out to encourage side shoots to develop, so creating a bushy specimen. Plants like bush fuchsias and chrysanthemums are stopped or pinched when they are about 15 cm (6 in) high. Sometimes the resultant side shoots are stopped to create really well-branched plants.

Supporting plants

In Chapter 4 I discussed the main methods of supporting plants such as climbers. So now let us look at the various materials available for tying in stems. The traditional material is raffia, which is suitable for even the softest stems. There is also plastic 'raffia' available which is almost as good, but not quite so soft. Soft garden string can also be recommended.

The usual method of tying in stems is to form a figure-of-eight loop around the cane (or other support) and the stem of the plant. Never tie in too tightly, for stems must have room to grow. If the ties are tight they will cut into the expanding stems and cause damage.

Split rings are also useful for tying in the stems of pot plants to split canes, a useful method of supporting plants with floppy stems, such as schizanthus. Alternatively, thin-stemmed pot plants could be supported with twiggy hazel sticks, pushed into the compost before the plants become too tall. They will then grow through the sticks and hide them.

Controlling pests and diseases

In a conservatory used for living in one cannot go around spraying everything with a pressure sprayer as one would in a greenhouse, in order to control pests and diseases. Nor can one use smoke cones for pest and disease control, although these are ideal for the conservatory devoted to plants.

It would be more practical to use an aerosol houseplant pest killer with a wide spectrum of activity. One such will eradicate pests like greenfly, red spider mites, whitefly, scale insects, mealy bugs and thrips.

To date there are no fungicides specifically for use in the home, so if any of your plants are infected with common fungal diseases such as mildew and grey mould (botrytis) then take them out in the garden and spray them thoroughly with benomyl fungicide. When dry take them back inside.

An excellent method of controlling two major pests under glass – whitefly and red spider mites – is biological control. With this method we introduce predatory or parasitic insects to keep the pests under control. These are supplied on leaves from specialist producers, and the leaves are placed among the plants. A good time to commence biological control is in early or mid-spring.

Introduce parasites or predators only when pests are found on the plants otherwise they will not survive because they will have nothing to live on – they do not feed on plants. And do not use insecticides with biological control or you will kill the beneficial creatures.

Red spider mites are controlled with the predatory mite *Phytoseiulus persimilis* and whitefly with the parasitic wasp *Encarsia formosa*.

General hygiene

The conservatory which is devoted purely to growing plants will need thoroughly cleaning out at least once a year. Due to frequent damping down of floor and staging, and perhaps spraying the structure and plants with a hosepipe to create humidity in hot weather, green algae and slime build up on all surfaces.

Ideally the conservatory should be completely emptied of plants and the inside scrubbed out with horticultural disinfectant. Clean the glass, framework, staging and floor. The green algae which build up in the glass overlaps can be removed by inserting a thin plastic plant label between the panes and then flushing out with a hosepipe. Finally forcefully wash down the structure with a hosepipe. Clean the outside, too, in the same way.

Shingle, gravel and so on, on benches and staging, can be washed in a sieve, using a hosepipe. This will get rid of any soil or compost which has washed down into it.

Before returning the plants it is a good idea to shut down the conservatory and light some smoke cones containing insecticide and fungicide to kill any remaining pests and diseases.

Of course, you cannot treat a living area in this way, but still it will need cleaning, perhaps not so much the framework, but certainly the glass. This must be kept clean at all times to allow maximum light transmission. There are horticultural glass cleaners available which not only remove green algae and grime, but leave the glass sparkling. The overlaps between the panes of glass can again be cleaned out with the help of a thin plastic plant label.

APPENDIX

A selection of U.K. conservatory manufacturers

Standard Designs

Baco Leisure Products Ltd, Windover Road, Huntingdon, PE18 7EH.

Banbury Homes and Gardens Ltd, P.O. Box 17, Banbury, Oxfordshire, OX17 3NS.

Crittall Warmlife Ltd, Crittall Road, Witham, Essex, CM8 3AW.

Eden Conservatories, Monarch Aluminium Ltd, Manor Road, Swindon Village, Cheltenham, Gloucestershire, GL51 9SQ.

Halls Homes and Gardens Ltd, Church Road, Paddock Wood, Tonbridge, Kent, TN12 6EU.

High Speed Glass, Dollar Street House, Dollar Street, Cirencester, Gloucestershire, GL7 2AP.

Marley Buildings Ltd, Peasmarsh, Guildford, Surrey, GU3 1LS.

Robinson's of Winchester Ltd, Robinson House, Winnall, Winchester, Hampshire, SO23 8LH.

Modular/Custom-made Designs

Alexander Bartholomew Conservatories Ltd, 277 Putney Bridge Road, London, SW15 2PT.

Alitex Ltd, Station Road, Alton, Hampshire, GU34 2PZ (also standard designs).

Amdega Ltd, Faverdale, Darlington, Co. Durham, DL3 0PW.

Classical Conservatories, Gardenvase Ltd, Unit 16C, Chalwyn Industrial Estate, St Clements Road, Poole, Dorset, BH15 3PE.

Crusader Conservatories Ltd, Neville Road, North Tees Industrial Estate, Stockton-on-Tees, Cleveland, TS18 2RD.

Machin Designs Ltd, Ransom's Dock, Parkgate Road, London, SW11 4NP.

Marston and Langinger, Hall Staithe, Fakenham, Norfolk, NR21 9BW.

Room Outside Ltd, Goodwood Gardens, Waterbeach, Nr. Chichester, West Sussex, PO18 0QB.

York Conservatories, Hull Road, Kexby, York, YO4 5LE.

A selection of U.S. garden room distributors

Aluminium Greenhouses Inc. 14605 Lorain Avenue, P.O. Box 11087, Cleveland, OH 44111.

Four Seasons Greenhouses, 425 Smith Street, Farmingdale, NY 11735.

Janco Greenhouses, 9390 Davis Avenue, Laurel, MD 20707.

Lord & Burnham Co. CSB 3181 Melville, NY 11747.

Machin Designs (USA) Inc. P.O. Box 167 Rowayton, CT 06853.

Santa Barbara Greenhouses, 1115J Avenida Acaso, Camarillo, CA 93010.

Sturdi-Built Mfg. Co. 11304 S.W. Boones Ferry Road, Portland, OR 97219.

Vegetable Factory/Solar Structures Div. Box 2235, New York, NY 11735.

INDEX